THE RUSSIAN REVOLUTIONS
OF 1917

JOHN SHELTON CURTISS

Professor of History
Duke University

AN ANVIL ORIGINAL
under the general editorship of
LOUIS L. SNYDER

D. VAN NOSTRAND COMPANY, INC.

PRINCETON, NEW JERSEY

TORONTO   LONDON

NEW YORK

TO EDNA SUTTER CURTISS

D. VAN NOSTRAND COMPANY, INC.

120 Alexander St., Princeton, New Jersey
257 Fourth Avenue, New York 10, New York
25 Hollinger Rd., Toronto 16, Canada
Macmillan & Co., Ltd., St. Martin's St.,
London, W.C. 2, England

*All correspondence should be addressed to the
principal office of the company at Princeton, N. J.*

COPYRIGHT, ©, 1957, BY
JOHN SHELTON CURTISS
Published simultaneously in Canada by
D. VAN NOSTRAND COMPANY (Canada), LTD.

Library of Congress Catalog Card No. 56-12901

PRINTED IN THE UNITED STATES OF AMERICA

PREFACE

THIS volume is intended to meet the needs of the student of modern world history, for whom the standard accounts of the Russian Revolutions of 1917 are too detailed. The aim has been to provide a treatment both compact and comprehensive. With this end in view, it begins with a brief background of the revolutions, starting with the Emancipation of 1861, and sketching in the major unsolved problems of Russia down to 1905. The period of the Duma, from 1905 to 1914, receives special emphasis, as does Russia's experience during the First World War. The revolutionary period is then analyzed in detail, with particular attention to the intense political struggle of 1917 and the economic and social factors that aided the fall of the moderate government and the rise of the Soviet regime. Little has been said about the international aspects of the revolutionary year, except as they affected events within Russia. The aim has been to strip the revolutionary struggle of non-essentials without over-simplifying to the point of inaccuracy.

The readings presented in the second part of the book have been chosen to shed light on aspects of the situation that are only lightly touched on in the body of the text. In particular, the leading actors have been permitted to express themselves in their own words, in hopes that they will lend vividness and clarify the personalities and the outlooks of the protagonists. Contemporary accounts also help to explain the psychology and the actions of the people.

The dates for events before 1917 are given according to the Julian calendar, which since 1900 has been thirteen days behind ours. The dates in 1917 and 1918, however, are given according to the Gregorian calendar. Thus the February revolution, which toppled the *Tsar*, actually happened in March of 1917, while the revolution of October 25, when the Bolsheviks took power, has its anniversary on November 7. The final date in the book is March 16, 1918, the day of the ratification of the Treaty of Brest-Litovsk. Although it was not a real turning-point in Soviet affairs, by that time the Soviet regime had achieved a measure of stability and had begun to display the main outlines of the features that have made it unique.

Duke University   JOHN S. CURTISS

TABLE OF CONTENTS

— 1 —

INTRODUCTION

The Russian Revolutions of 1917 were not an isolated outburst, but were rather the culmination of a struggle of large parts of the Russian people to secure redress for their accumulated grievances. Ever since the freeing of the serfs in 1861, revolutionary movements had sought with little success to compel the government to reform a still backward regime. In 1905 the hardships of the war with Japan touched off a powerful revolutionary explosion that forced the Tsar to make significant concessions, which, however, he much reduced after the revolutionary blast had spent its force. The Duma, which first met in 1906, achieved little in the way of basic reform. Thus the Russian empire entered the First World War with its fundamental problems unsolved. The terrible calamities of the war intensified the impact of these problems and caused the fall of the Tsar.

There were two distinct revolutions in 1917. The first, known as the February Revolution (although it was in March, according to our calendar), was a spontaneous, moderate affair, which sought chiefly to replace the incompetent government of the Tsar with a more effective one of progressive political leaders. Because its program was to leave the existing social and economic system intact and to pursue policies espoused by the middle class, the socialists dubbed it a "bourgeois" government, produced by a "bourgeois" rather than a "proletarian" revolution. To be sure, this bourgeois government at times consisted largely of members of moderate socialist parties, with few members of the bourgeoisie included. Nevertheless, be-

cause its policy favored moderate political reform rather
than radical social change, in socialist parlance it has
always been known as a bourgeois revolution. The second
upheaval of 1917 was the October Revolution.

The October Revolution, whose anniversary is now
marked on November 7, was a farreaching social revolution, organized and led by the Bolsheviks, the radical party
headed by Lenin. At first Lenin and his party had an
insignificant following, but the reluctance of the new
Provisional Government to end the war as the masses
wished, and the postponement of agrarian reform, gave
Lenin his chance to win wide support in the army and
among the urban proletariat and some of the peasants. By
profiting by the mistakes of both the conservatives and
the moderate socialists, Lenin and the Bolsheviks were
able to muster overwhelming strength against their opponents, headed by Kerensky, whom they overthrew with
ease. They then set up the Soviet government on November 8, 1917.

Once installed, the new Soviet regime acted with decision and dispatch upon the problems that it faced. The
peasants, already on the march, were encouraged to take
the land of the landowners for their own use, and other
sweeping measures were adopted. When the moderate
socialists proved unwilling to enter a coalition government
with the Bolsheviks except upon their own terms, Lenin
scornfully pushed them aside and formed a predominantly
Bolshevik government, avowedly the dictatorship of the
proletariat. The Constituent Assembly, which met in
January, 1918, was forcibly dispersed because its moderate
members refused to accept the leadership of the new
Soviet government. Centers of armed opposition to the
regime were soon overcome by Red forces, while a political police was created to terrorize less overt opposition.
Finally, after long negotiations, the war with Germany
was brought to an end. To be sure, this was only at the
cost of staggering territorial losses; nevertheless, by the
end of March, 1918, the Soviet government stood apparently secure and at peace. Actually, long years of grim
trials and sufferings lay ahead; but the Bolshevik or Communist Revolution was now inscribed on the pages of
history.

THE BACKGROUND OF THE REVOLUTIONS OF 1917

The Emancipation of 1861. While the origins of the Russian peasant problem lie several centuries ago, for the background of the revolutions of 1917 it is enough to go back only to 1861, when the serfs were liberated by the reforming Tsar, Alexander II. Earlier rulers had gingerly approached the problem without doing anything basic about it. Alexander II, however, conservative though he was, realized that the rising tide of peasant revolts, especially during the Crimean War (1853-1856), would not permit further delay. As he told the nobility: "Better to abolish serfdom from above than to wait until it abolishes itself from below." Consequently, he was able to prod and nag the nobility into setting the conditions for the emancipation.

Unlike the Negro slaves in the United States, the Russian serfs were freed with land, for which they had to make redemption payments to the government for forty-nine years. The government in turn paid the landowners. (The house serfs were freed without land and without payments.) While there were endless local variations in the terms, in general it can be said that the peasants of the main farming areas of the south and center, where the land was valuable, received substantially less land than they had had before the Emancipation. They, however, had to pay only a moderate premium above its market value. The much smaller numbers of peasants in the poor farming areas of the north were given plenty of the less valuable land of the region, but had to pay about double its worth. This was because in the north the peasants had supported themselves in part by nonagricultural activities (handicrafts, or wage-work in the cities). Their masters in turn had drawn upon both agricultural and nonagricultural incomes of their serfs. For this reason they set the rates of the redemption payments high enough to compensate for the loss of both types of income. Thus, the peasants had cause to complain: in the south because they received small parcels of land, at not too exorbitant prices; in the north, because of the extremely high payments. They rioted in protest: in 1861 some 1,176 outbreaks were reported, with smaller numbers in 1862 and 1863. The government broke the resistance with the use of troops, by shooting, exiling, and flogging. But the peasants always held the conviction that they had been robbed and that someday they would get all of the landowners' land, on the principle that he that worked the land should own it.

The Growth of the Revolutionary Movement.   Alexander II introduced other important reforms after the Emancipation. In 1864 he set up a highly progressive system of courts and created elected local governmental units called *zemstvos*. He liberalized the censorship and the educational system, provided representative city government, and set up a modernized military system. But early in his reign, liberals and radicals protested bitterly against the unfairness of the Emancipation, and as the Tsar swung to conservatism, organized revolutionary movements appeared, with the Land and Liberty Society in 1862. For some time little was done by the revolutionaries. Later, many students, infuriated by harsh measures of repression, joined the radicals in the work of propaganda, first in the factories, and then in 1873, among the peasants.

The movement of the revolutionaries "to the people" accomplished little, as the disguises assumed by the radicals were unconvincing, and both peasants and police were suspicious. After the inevitable arrests and punishments, the Land and Liberty Society lost hope of arousing a peasant uprising in the near future. Many of them turned to terrorism against high officials of the Tsar, and when several such killings failed to bring about the desired revolution, they made the Tsar himself the target. In 1879 the terrorists formed a new society, "The Will of the People," and openly proclaimed their intention to kill Alexander. Seven attempts with high explosives ended with his death in March, 1881, just after he had signed a decree providing for limited public participation in legislative procedure.

The Reaction Under Alexander III. The murder of
Alexander II failed to cause the expected revolution. Instead, Alexander III embarked on a program of stern
repression. His father's assassins were rounded up and
hanged, while the police with redoubled vigor stamped
out the revolutionary movement. This was soon achieved,
but at the price of indiscriminate exiling of many, among
them innocent men, merely upon suspicion. The reaction
also embraced the educational system. The universities
were purged, and the lower schools also were under harsh
control. Strong efforts were made to have the elementary
schools of the *zemstvos* converted into parochial schools,
although without success. The *zemstvos* themselves, however, were subject to severe restrictions. As for the
peasants, they were now at the mercy of appointed officials
known as land captains who had wide powers over them.
Representative government and the civil liberties appeared
farther off than ever, and the accession of Nicholas II in
1894 offered little reason for hope.

But while there was retrogression in political life,
Russian industry spurted under Alexander III and
Nicholas II. Stimulated by large injections of French and
other capital and aided by favorable tariff policies, the
existing textile industry grew rapidly, especially around
Moscow, while the coal fields of the Donets Basin of the
Ukraine became the basis for a booming iron and steel
industry. Extensive railroad building consumed large
amounts of steel. A beet-sugar industry sprang up around
Kiev, and at Baku in the Caucasus Russian oil wells
challenged the United States for first place. Foreign in-
vestors and the small Russian capitalist class made substantial profits from industry. At the same time, in the
factories there was formed a working class, made sullen
by extremely long hours, low pay, and harsh treatment by
employers.

Agriculture, on the other hand, was not prosperous.
Russia poured forth upon the markets of the world great
quantities of wheat, but at heavy cost to the peasants.
Burdened by redemption dues upon their land and by
heavy taxes, and kept in ignorance by a grossly inadequate
school system, most of the peasants were unable to pay
their way. Although delinquents were severely flogged, by
1900 the peasants were in arrears by one full year's quota

of redemption dues. Repeated official investigations called attention to their hopeless situation, which was brought to light by an especially severe famine in 1891-1892. Although the amount of land per peasant decreased somewhat because the population rose rapidly after the Emancipation, the poverty of the peasants was chiefly caused by extremely unproductive farming methods. They had far larger holdings of land than the French or German peasants, but their crop yields were much lower, thanks to wooden plows, sickles for harvesting, and the medieval three-field system, which left one-third of the plow-land idle every year.

Given the ignorance of the peasants and their system of communal landholding, intensive agriculture was largely out of the question. Instead, the one remedy that the peasant saw for his poverty was more land, to be obtained by taking over the estates of the nobility. This, of course, the government rigorously opposed. Thus, the peasants, like the factory workers, were potential trouble-makers, although, unlike the workers, they rarely expressed their discontent by action.

The Rise of Opposition Parties.   Political parties, illegal in Russia, appeared at the end of the nineteenth century, largely as a result of the famine of 1891 and the cholera epidemic that followed it. The evidence of the terrible poverty of the peasants aroused intellectuals to seek to remedy their ills, for which there were no legal channels. Those who leaned toward Marxism turned enthusiasically to the workers, who had begun to engage in stubborn strikes. Marxism had come to Russia largely through the efforts of George Plekhanov, an exiled member of the old Land and Liberty Society. At first it had appealed chiefly to intellectuals, but in 1895 under the leadership of Vladimir Ilich Ulianov, known as Lenin, and Julius Martov, the Marxists sought to incite the workers. In 1898 delegates from several of the local Marxist organizations met at Minsk to organize the Russian Social Democratic Party, only to be promptly arrested. Lenin and Plekhanov continued the movement with the publication of a newspaper, *Iskra* (*The Spark*), which was smuggled into Russia from Germany.

In 1903 the Social Democrats held a congress at London, at which splits in the party became evident.

Lenin, who demanded a small, highly disciplined party of professional revolutionaries to lead the masses, was defeated by Martov, who stood for a large party open to all active supporters. The withdrawal of the Jewish Bund group, however, gave Lenin's faction a majority of the congress, for which reason they were dubbed the Bolsheviks (majority men), while Martov's group received the name of Mensheviks (men of the minority). Although the split in the party was patched up, it continued to grow. Led by Lenin, the Bolsheviks were a group of uncompromising revolutionaries, while the Mensheviks, with Martov and Plekhanov, leaned toward the milder, nonrevolutionary tactics of the German Social Democrats.

In 1901 the Socialist Revolutionaries organized under the leadership of G. A. Gershuni and Victor Chernov. Their program, while somewhat similar to that of the Social Democrats, differed in its strong peasant orientation and its willingness to work with the liberal bourgeoisie against the government of the Tsar. They were a purely Russian party and opposed international, centralized state socialism. And, unlike the Social Democrats, they used terroristic assassination of officials as well as propaganda to promote their ends.

Organization of the Liberals. The liberals of Russia also became active around the turn of the century. After participating in the famine relief in 1891 and 1892, liberal *zemstvo* members ought to obtain representative government by petitioning the crown, only to be roundly snubbed. Similarly, professional men, many of them employed by the *zemstvos*, organized into professional unions and voiced political demands. Stern opposition from the government failed to deter them, and *zemstvo* congresses after 1901 kept alive the constitutional movement. An illegal newspaper, *Liberation*, was smuggled into Russia, and in 1903 the underground Union of Liberation was formed to unite *zemstvo* liberals and the professional men, who were led by P. N. Miliukov and P. B. Struve.

Thus, for the first time, the imperial regime was faced by a significant organized opposition, as well as by an increasingly radical student movement. Assassination of high government officials by Socialist Revolutionaries, long and bitter strikes of factory workers led by Social

Democrats, and peasant disorders in the Ukraine showed the extent of the movement, which the severe repressive measures of V. K. von Plehve could not subdue. The situation continued to get worse, until Plehve is alleged to have said that the country could be saved from revolution only by a short, victorious war.

The Russo-Japanese War. In 1895 the Russian government began to seek predominance in the Far East in defiance of Japan. Led by unscrupulous adventurers, the Tsar seized a base at Port Arthur in Manchuria and pushed into Korea, in spite of Japanese protests and offers to compromise. Finally, convinced that the Russians would not turn aside, the Japanese in February, 1904, began the Russo-Japanese war with a surprise torpedo attack on the Russian fleet, which gave them supremacy on the sea. Japanese armies then poured into Korea and Manchuria and forced the Russians back, while laying siege to Port Arthur. The Russians lost one battle after another, and when Port Arthur finally fell, the Japanese massed for attack on the Russians at Mukden. Here, also, the Japanese were victorious, and the Russians retreated to the north, hoping for salvation by a naval victory. The Russian Baltic Fleet had sailed around Africa and Asia to the Far East to win naval supremacy, but on May 14, 1905, in a short battle at Tsushima it was annihilated. Both Russia and Japan were now ready for peace, which, thanks to the mediation of President Theodore Roosevelt, was made at Portsmouth, N. H., in July, 1905. Russia lost little but her claims on South Manchuria and Korea. Nevertheless, the imperial regime had suffered a resounding defeat in a war that had been unpopular from the start. Far from smothering the revolutionary fires, this war fanned the flames.

The Revolution of 1905. At the beginning of the Japanese war, patriotic fervor moderated the opposition to the government, but the latter's unwillingness to allow the *zemstvos* to help and, above all, the defeats, soon revived it. For many, the autocracy was a worse enemy than the Japanese. The hated Plehve, assassinated in August, 1904, was replaced by the moderate Sviatopolk-Mirsky, who relaxed the oppressive regime. But his relaxations were not enough to satisfy the aroused opposition, and the milder police measures aided the radical groups. The embattled liberals agitated strongly in favor of civil liberties and a representative assembly, which most hoped would have legislative powers. The Tsar, however, was unwilling to grant this.

The fall of Port Arthur in December, 1904, further stimulated the opposition, but was far overshadowed by the events of Bloody Sunday. On January 9, 1905, long columns of striking workers of St. Petersburg, with their families and carrying ikons and religious banners, marched under the leadership of Father George Gapon to present their petition to the Tsar at the Winter Palace. They were met by strong forces of troops, which opened fire, killing and wounding hundreds. This outrage infuriated the public, and demonstrations, strikes, assassinations, and other forms of violence shook the regime. The universities closed for seven months. The Tsar was especially shaken by the killing of his uncle, the Grand Duke Sergei, military commander of Moscow, on February 4.

Soon afterward Nicholas issued decrees promising concessions, among them a limited form of popular representation. But these gestures were insufficient to satisfy the Union of Liberation and the newly formed Union of Unions, led by Professor Miliukov. *Zemstvo* conferences, meeting in defiance of the police, also demanded basic reforms. The defeats at Mukden and Tsushima hardened public opinion, and riots, strikes, agrarian disorders, and assassinations grew ever more frequent. Troops battled strikers in Lodz, a general strike seized Odessa, and on June 14 the warship Potemkin of the Black Sea fleet put out to sea under control of her mutinous crew. The reactionary supporters of the Tsar fought back by forming the ultra-conservative Union of the Russian People, which loosed bands of thugs upon the Jewish population in a series of frightful pogroms or riots, often with the toleration of the authorities. These excesses infuriated liberals and radicals and did nothing for the prestige of the autocracy.

Additional conciliatory gestures by the Tsar failed to restore order, as endless political meetings filled the university halls, where, thanks to the grant of autonomy, the police might not enter. In October, a series of strikes in Moscow and St. Petersburg swelled into a general strike

that paralyzed the country. Revolutionary mobs roamed
the streets, carrying posters attacking the government
and demanding a democratic republic. In St. Petersburg
full control of the city was in the hands of the Soviet, an
elected body of the masses, with Trotsky as its active
leader. Soviets also appeared in Moscow and other cities,
and barricades rose in many towns.

The October Manifesto. Nicholas II, faced with
this crisis, wavered between repression and concessions.
As Trepov, his strong man, who earlier had commanded:
"Don't spare the cartridges!" had failed to restore order,
it was the turn of S. Iu. Witte. After making peace with
Japan he had returned to Russia in time to be called in
by the desperate Tsar. Witte offered the Tsar two choices:
either a military dictatorship under someone else, or a
constitutional regime. The Grand Duke Nicholas, on
whom the Tsar called for dictatorial measures, refused
in tears, so that the Tsar perforce had to turn to Witte.
The result was the Manifesto of October 17, which
provided for the civil liberties, an extremely wide fran-
chise, and the "immutable rule" that no legislation would
be promulgated without the consent of the Duma, which
should also have control over state officials.

The Tsar's Manifesto achieved its purpose. While reactionaries shuddered and revolutionaries warned that the
concession was a trick, the liberals accepted the reforms
as a basis for further negotiations, and many of the
zemstvo men expressed complete satisfaction. The de-
lirious public rejoicing was soon cooled, however, by a
number of ferocious pogroms of the Union of the Russian
People, who took out their wrath upon the Jews. It was
some time before life returned to normal. Mass demonstrations, and in some places civil war, swept the border
lands; military and naval units mutinied; the St. Petersburg Soviet again called for a general strike; in Moscow
an armed uprising led by the Bolsheviks produced a week
of bloody street fighting.

But the revolutionary wave had spent most of its
strength, and as reliable troops returned from Manchuria
the government could send out punitive detachments to
flog and hang the recalcitrants. In the last months of 1905
a wave of fierce peasant disorders looted and burned over

two thousand manor houses, but, thereafter, the repression gained the upper hand. The country began to look to the Duma to remedy its grievances.

The First Duma. In the months after the October Manifesto, Witte was busy revising the Fundamental Laws of the Empire to make a place for the new Duma. In so doing he whittled away many of the earlier concessions. An upper house, the Council of State, half appointed by the crown, would serve as a check upon the people's representatives in the Duma. The Duma was deprived of power to control the budget, of power over army and navy and foreign affairs. Moreover, under Article 87 of the Fundamental Laws, the crown had the power to issue decrees when the legislature was not in session, although the decrees had to be validated later when it was again meeting. Finally, the procedure for electing the Duma was made indirect and very complicated, and the voting was weighted heavily in favor of landowners and wealthy townsmen against peasants and workers. After this task had been completed, Witte, long hated by the Tsar and the Empress, was dismissed. The key figure in 1906 was P. A. Stolypin, Minister of Interior, who had displayed courage and determination as governor of a rebellious province.

Much to the annoyance of the government, the elections to the Duma failed to provide a conciliatory majority. Although the parties of the Left had boycotted the elections, when the Duma met on April 27, 1906, the Constitutional Democrats, formed out of the Union of Liberation and the Union of Unions by Miliukov, proved to be the largest party, and enjoyed the support of several of the others. The Cadets, as this party was known, favored using the Duma to transform Russia into a limited monarchy on the British pattern. To satisfy the peasants, the Cadets proposed to compel the landowners to cede much of their land to the peasants for moderate compensation—a measure strongly opposed by the Tsar. Inevitably the Duma and the government, which proposed no program of its own, quarreled furiously. Eventually, when the Duma was on the point of passing its land measure, on July 9, 1906 the government ordered its dissolution. The Second Duma was to convene on February 20, 1907.

The Second Duma. The flouting of public opinion by the dismissal of the Duma produced a new wave of mutinies, terroristic acts, and peasant uprisings, but Stolypin was able to crush the revolts by sending out punitive expeditions, which used field courts-martial to impose summary penalties. As a result, the noose won the nickname of "Stolypin's necktie." The success of the repressive measures encouraged the government to hope for election of a more moderate Second Duma. But while the Cadets lost heavily in the voting, many of the votes went to the parties of the Left, including a vehement group of Bolsheviks. Hence, when the Second Duma met on February 20, 1907, it, the most truly representative of the Dumas, was very stormy.

The Cadets, although considerably weakened, again assumed the leadership of the Duma. They were now much more conservative than formerly, as they feared that the Tsar might abolish the Duma entirely, and hence they sought to pass progressive legislation without giving too great offense to the Tsar. The Bolsheviks had other ideas. Their intention was to discredit the Duma in the eyes of the people by showing that it could not deal with their real grievances, and further to discredit the Cadets and the moderate socialists as appeasers of the autocracy. Time and time again they returned to the attack with sweeping charges—against the army, against the police, against the imperial taxation system. In this way they mobilized peasant opinion against the government and forced the Cadets to intervene to stop the attacks. In spite of the noisy interruptions, the Cadets managed to advance considerable legislation, including a moderate agrarian bill. This the government did not want passed, and, bitterly annoyed with the Duma, sought a pretext to dissolve it and make sweeping changes in the voting laws. It found the pretext by making unproven charges against the Social Democratic members of attempting to subvert the army. When the Duma wanted to consider the charges before permitting the arrest of its members, Stolypin, already provided with a decree of dissolution, sent the Duma home. A new election law was immediately promulgated on June 3, 1907, without the consent of the legislature.

The Third and Fourth Dumas. The new election

law grossly favored the landowners and discriminated against peasants and workers, with the result that the Third Duma was dominated by the conservatives and did not represent the popular will. But when it assembled in November, 1907, the revolutionary movement had collapsed and the public was in no mood for further violence. The radical leaders had fled abroad or were sent into exile, and peasants and workers sank into sullen apathy. Thus, the Third Duma was able to last out its full five-year term. It followed a strongly nationalist course, oppressing Finns, Jews, and Ukrainians. Its most valuable activity was to promote public education through liberal grants of funds, so that the goal of universal education became visible in the distance. The army and the navy were rebuilt and reformed, in order that Russia might again play the role of a great power.

Nothing was done, however, to satisfy the eternal peasant demand for the land of the nobility. Instead, in 1910, the Duma passed Stolypin's measure for giving the peasant individual ownership of his land by breaking up the village commune. This measure, which might well have enabled some of the peasants to prosper through individual initiative, actually accomplished little because of the shortness of the time for it to take effect, and the peasants remained miserably poor. Also the industrial workers found that their lot improved little, in spite of boom times in industry after 1909. Social legislation passed by the Duma failed to mollify them, and a major strike movement developed from 1912 to 1914, almost assuming revolutionary proportions in the latter year.

Stolypin, who dominated the Third Duma, failed to live to see the Fourth, as he was assassinated on September 1, 1911. His place was taken by V. N. Kokovtsov, a conservative bureaucrat. He succeeded in getting along rather well with the Third and the even more conservative Fourth Duma, although he was embarrassed by the disclosure of the influence over the Orthodox church enjoyed by the depraved Gregory Rasputin. The opposition aroused by the scandal of Rasputin was too slight, however, to shake the stability of the imperial government, and in August, 1914, Russia entered World War I apparently stronger than ever.

— 3 —

THE RUSSIAN EMPIRE IN THE FIRST WORLD WAR

Background of the War. For much of the nineteenth century, Russia and Germany had been friendly. After 1890, however, they pulled apart, as Russian interests in the Balkans conflicted with those of Austria-Hungary, Germany's ally. In 1894, Russia and France signed a defensive alliance directed against Germany, cemented by large French loans to Russia. Even after this, Russia and Germany remained fairly friendly until about 1906. In 1908 they came closer to war over the Bosnian incident. Russia, balked in her hopes to gain control of the Straits and Constantinople, strongly resented Austria's annexation of Bosnia, which was coveted by Russia's ally Serbia. Only a German ultimatum compelled Russia to recognize the annexation. Again, during the Balkan wars of 1912-1913, when Austria feverishly sought to limit Serbia's expansion, Russian anger grew. Fresh wrath against the Central powers was also aroused by Germany's efforts to strengthen the Turkish army in 1913. In Russia, as in Austria-Hungary and Germany, a belligerent spirit was growing in influential circles.

In June, 1914, when the Austrian Archduke Francis Ferdinand was assassinated with the complicity of Serbian terrorists, the Russian government at first warned the Serbs to make amends. But when Austria-Hungary presented an ultimatum apparently designed to lead to war against Serbia, and when Vienna quickly declared war, Russia sought to protect her small ally against the Austrians. The Russians began partial mobilization against Austria, but then, under pressure from his generals, the Tsar reluctantly agreed to full mobilization, knowing that this might well lead Germany to declare war. Germany did so on July 19/August 1, 1914. From a Balkan quarrel the war had become a general one.

The First Months of the War. When war came, Russia was stronger than ever before. There was considerable popular support for the government, and political conflict almost vanished. The Duma, in an outburst of patriotism, voted full support and gave the government a free hand. The people responded well to the call for mobilization. Even most of the socialists gave their support. As for the Bolshevik group in the Duma, who sharply opposed the war, it was quickly arrested and exiled to Siberia.

The Russian army, thoroughly reorganized after the Japanese war, had more artillery and machine guns than before, and an excellent spirit. But, in spite of belief in victory in a few months, the army was poorly prepared to fight the best military power in the world. The Russians had far fewer guns per division than the Germans, and no heavy field guns. Even worse, the Russians, with feeble facilities for making ammunition, had only 1,000 shell per gun, while the Germans had 3,000 per gun and ample capacity to make more. The Russians were also woefully lacking in machine guns, with only 4,100 in the whole army. Their supply and medical system were primitive (*see Reading No. 1*), their communications weak, and their aviation was far inferior to the Germans. Against the Austrians the Russians could more than hold their own, but from the beginning the Germans far outclassed them.

Even more disastrous, the Russian high command was poorly organized. It was only on the second day that the Grand Duke Nicholas, uncle of the Tsar, was named commander-in-chief, much to his surprise. He himself stated that at first he wept copiously because he did not know how to perform his new duties. Although he had some success, his appointment was unfortunate. His chief-of-staff, General Ianushkevich, had had no field experience, and other high commanders were also poorly trained. V. A. Sukhomlinov, the Minister of War, was either extremely incompetent or a traitor. Moreover, the Russian leaders were still steeped in the maxims of Suvorov, Catherine the Great's famous general, who had relied on the bayonet and scorned musket fire. These tactics, which had worked well in the eighteenth century, were obviously not suitable for 1914. But some Russian generals sneered at modern military science, which they termed "the ideas of an old professor." Sukhomlinov boasted that for twenty-five years he had not read a book on military affairs.

The Russians, who were slow to mobilize their great army, had intended to fight chiefly against the Austrians. Soon, however, hard-pressed France sent them urgent calls to attack the Germans. In response, the Russians improvised an East Prussian offensive, with armies under Samsonov and Rennenkampf to trap the weak German forces between them. But the two generals, bitter personal enemies since 1905, failed to cooperate. Against Samsonov, struggling up from the south through the difficult Masurian Lakes, Hindenburg, recalled from retirement, struck with the massed guns of his smaller force and annihilated the invaders. Later Rennenkampf was driven back across the border.

In all, the Russians lost some 300,000 men and 650 guns, and from this time their awe of the German military machine was great. Later, the Russians defeated a German attempt to capture Warsaw, but they allow a German force to escape almost certain capture, so the Germans retained their superiority. On the Austrian front, however, the Russians won a series of great victories that brought the Austrians to the verge of collapse and won almost all of Galicia. Even after the Germans had re-enforced the Austrians, the Russians continued their attacks well into the winter of 1914-1915.

The Russian Disasters of 1915. By the spring of 1915 the Russians, in spite of heavy losses, had pushed to the crest of the Carpathians and even through some of the passes to the Hungarian plain. The Russians depended chiefly upon the bayonet, as their ammunition was almost gone. With their extended lines and almost silent cannon the Russians invited a German counter-stroke, which came suddenly in April, 1915. With massed guns and heavy air attacks the Teutons cut the Russian army to pieces, whole units surrendering in confusion. The Germans pursued relentlessly, striking along the whole front, and threatened to entrap the Russians in Poland. The Russian cannon were limited at best to one shell per gun per day. Even the infantry lacked rifle ammunition, and reserve troops often had no rifles, but were forced to

lie unarmed under fire until the rifles of the killed and
wounded could be made available. (*See Reading No. 2.*)
Yet the Russian army held together under these demoral-
izing conditions, and late in the fall the Germans halted
their offensive on a line running from just west of Riga
to the corner of Galicia.

Naturally, the Russian losses during this period were
immense. At the height of the German drive, the killed
and wounded numbered 235,000 per month, and 200,000
prisoners were lost each month. During 1915 alone, the
Russians lost some 2,000,000 men killed and wounded,
and 1,300,000 prisoners, bringing the total losses since
the outbreak of the war to 4,360,000. It is no wonder that
the British General Knox, who was with the Russian
forces, stated that the army had come through a trial that
"would have been fatal to most armies." The remnants of
the army, although replenished in numbers, were inferior
in quality, as the great quantities of regular officers and
noncoms put out of action could never be replaced. Moreover, the morale of the Russians never could be restored.

Political Results of the Defeats.   Inevitably, news of
the difficulties of the army filtered back to the Duma as
early as January, 1915. At that time the members sharply
questioned Sukhomlinov, the Minister of War, only to be
told that the supply situation was satisfactory. The Duma
could do nothing, even though it was sure that this answer
was untrue. The leading political figures of the country
met and repeatedly urged basic reforms in the government,
only to be snubbed by the Tsar. The movement for reform
grew, however, and early in the summer of 1915 two-thirds
of the Duma organized the Progressive Bloc, headed by
P. N. Miliukov, to ask necessary reforms and the "Ministry of Confidence" that was so widely demanded. When
the Duma reconvened on June 19, 1915, there was a fierce
attack upon the reactionary and incompetent ministers,
who had opposed the mobilization of the public forces to
support the war. As a result, the Tsar replaced three of the
worst with able and respected conservatives. Sukhomlinov,
Minister of War, was also under attack, led by the able
and respected A. I. Guchkov. The Minister was so vulnerable to charges of incompetence and even treason
that Nicholas removed him in midsummer, amid general
rejoicing, and replaced him with the greatly admired

General A. A. Polivanov. The hopes of the Progressive Bloc were high.

The Sway of Rasputin.   The Empress Alexandra, a fanatical believer in the autocratic power of the Emperor, had long been under the influence of Rasputin, who urged her to combat the progressive tendencies. She had already expressed her hatred of Guchkov. In August, she and Rasputin persuaded the Tsar to dismiss the Grand Duke Nicholas, the commander-in-chief, and go to the front and take command himself. When the news leaked out, there was general consternation in the Duma, as the Tsar had no military training. Moreover, his absence from Petrograd would leave the government without a head. The feeling grew so strong that the ministers, under strong pressure from the Duma and the general public, on August 21 sent the Tsar a joint letter urging him to reconsider his decision. Only the aged Goremykin, the submissive Premier, opposed the protest. The letter, however, failed to deter the Tsar, who left for Headquarters on August 23. The ministers did not learn of his departure until two days later. By this act Nicholas cut himself off from the ministers. In reality, he turned over his political powers to the Empress, whom he encouraged to dabble in matters of state. The Empress, in turn, was firmly under the influence of Rasputin. And, thus, the great empire was dominated by a debauched and ignorant peasant, with whom no decent man could cooperate. The Empress, trusting firmly in him, threw herself into the work of running the state with dire results. The doom of the Empire was sealed.

The Brusilov Offensive in 1916.   In spite of the fatal turn in political life, the Russian army made a remarkable recovery over the winter of 1915-1916. The troops were rested and re-equipped, and heavy contingents of new men were added to the ranks. Thanks to the valuable work of Polivanov and Guchkov, and the efforts of the general public, the output of munitions increased greatly, while considerable quantities of supplies were obtained abroad. Thanks to these measures, the Russian army in 1916 was better equipped and provisioned than it had been since the outbreak of the war, and morale seemed high. Actually, however, the Russians were still far inferior to the foe in cannon and machine guns, and especially so in airplanes. In fact, as the German army also had improved greatly since 1914, the improved Russian army was even more inferior to the Germans than before. None the less, it was decided to take the offensive in 1916, to relieve the Allies, hard pressed in France, and especially to succor the Italians after the rout at Caporetto.

The Russian commanders facing the Germans had little hope of success, but Brusilov, commander in Galicia, was sure of success against the Austrians and was given command of the offensive. Thanks to effective artillery fire and numerical superiority, the Russians quickly overwhelmed the Austrians on a wide front and captured 400,000 prisoners. But with German aid the Austrians again halted the Russians with heavy losses. The Russians had diverted large German forces from France and had saved Italy. Moreover, Brusilov's success had finally lured Rumania into the war on the allied side—although Rumania soon experienced disaster. But in spite of these successes, the offensive was unwise. In 1916 the Russians lost more than 2,000,000 men killed and wounded, and 350,000 prisoners. Even more important, the morale of the Russian army was ruined beyond repair, and its collapse seemed certain. The army was ripe for revolution.

Ministerial Leapfrog. After the Tsar had gone to the front, the internal situation worsened rapidly. The country's economy began to display alarming signs of weakness. Inflation, slow at first, soon gained momentum, and prices soared. For the swollen populations of the cities this brought great hardship, as wages, pitifully low at best, lost their purchasing power. The misery of the working people was intensified by a growing shortage of food. The peasants found it unprofitable to sell their grain for inflated money, especially as there were few manufactured goods to buy with it. In addition, the railroads proved unable to cope with the enormous problem of supplying the huge army as well as the civilian population, and often available food supplies could not be transported. Food riots and strikes became more frequent, although the government dealt severely with the participants. A fuel shortage added to the woes of the urban inhabitants. As for the peasants, they were fairly docile, but they were more and more disgusted with the war, which had taken so many of their men and was constantly taking more.

Under these circumstances, able administration was imperative. It was not, however, supplied. Instead, the Empress, egged on by Rasputin, campaigned for the removal of the able men appointed by the Tsar in the summer of 1915. Two of them were dismissed in September, and a few months later two others went. Polivanov, the capable Minister of War, was especially hated by the Empress, who wrote to her husband: "A greater traitor than Sukhomlinov." (*See Reading No. 3.*) When Nicholas finally gave in and removed him, she wrote: "Oh, the relief! Now I can sleep well." More and more the reputable men of Russia found it impossible to work under the influence of Rasputin, who, steeped in debauchery, was surrounded by a crowd of unprincipled adventurers. During the last eighteen months of the empire, the public was regaled with the spectacle of the "ministerial leap-frog," as one corrupt politician succeeded another in the positions of power, while Rasputin pulled the strings. In December, 1915, Nicholas removed old Goremykin because of his inability to cope with the strong opposition to him. His successor, however, was Stürmer, a shady and disreputable politician for whom nobody had a good word. This appointment caused consternation at home and abroad, as he was incorrectly believed to be pro-German. He kept his post for almost a year. At first he posed as a friend of the Duma, to the great delight of the public.

But as the governmental scandals grew ever more noisome, and as the inability of the administration to deal with the food situation became more obvious, public opinion grew more and more vehement against Stürmer's government. Finally, the naming of A. D. Protopopov as Minister of Interior outraged Duma and public alike. Even the Tsar protested against him, but the urging of the Empress and Rasputin won out. It was not long before Protopopov's proven connections with Rasputin infuriated the citizenry, while his unbalanced mental state made him obviously unfit for the key post of Minister of Interior. Feeling ran so high that he did not dare appear before the Duma, over which he had once presided. In November, 1916, the Tsar decided to dismiss him, but the Empress in despair fought for him, and Protopopov remained in power until the end.

The Rising Tide of Unrest. Protopopov failed signally in his efforts to control the situation. In October, 1916, he sought to smash a city-wide strike in Petrograd by using two regiments of the garrison to reinforce the police. The troops, however, fired, not on the strikers, but on the police—an ominous note. Reports from the front frequently stressed that the soldiers wanted only peace and bread. Opposition to the war was so great that some officers feared to lead their troops in action lest they be shot by their own men. Protests demanding basic reforms were adopted by the *zemstvos* and the town governments, by the financial interests, by the nobility, and countless other organized groups. The situation grew so menacing that members of the Tsar's family met in secret to consider deposing the Tsar and the Empress as a means of avoiding the coming revolution. Generals and members of the Duma conferred concerning similar action, but nobody dared to take the lead.

On November 1, 1916, the Duma met for the first time in five months. Miliukov, leader of the Progressive Bloc, delivered a scathing attack on "the dark forces" around the throne, ending each part of his indictment with the question: "Is this stupidity or is it treason?" He was followed by several of the conservatives, who furiously denounced Rasputin and Stürmer. The latter, terrified, dared not challenge the Duma, in spite of the great wrath of the Empress. For once the Tsar acted independently by dismissing Stürmer and replacing him with a decent man, who insisted on removing Protopopov. The frantic Empress went to Headquarters, however, and secured the Tsar's promise to keep him, so that the dismissal of Stürmer brought little improvement. Fresh speeches in the Duma condemning Rasputin and his henchmen showed the enormous dissatisfaction of the Russian educated public, but produced no change in the government. The only result was further to infuriate the Empress, who demanded that the Tsar dismiss the Duma. "Russia loves to feel the whip."

One consequence of the speeches in the Duma was that several of the highest nobility of Russia decided to assassinate Rasputin in order to save the regime. Prince Yusupov, related to the Tsar by marriage, and the Grand Duke Dimitry, nephew of the Tsar, plied Rasputin with poisoned wine, and when that failed to take effect, he was shot and his body dumped into the river. When the corpse was recovered, the Tsar and the Empress attended his funeral upon the palace grounds. Rasputin's removal had no effect upon the political life of the land, which continued to drift toward revolution.

— 4 —

THE FIRST REVOLUTIONARY MONTHS

The Mounting Crisis. In the first two months of 1917, dissatisfaction in Russia grew rapidly. The inflation advanced at a fast pace, with severe effects upon the working population, which showed its exasperation by an increasing number of strikes. The food shortages angered all, especially the women who had to wait in line for hours in the bitter cold, sometimes to find that there was no food to be had. In the rising popular fury the radical parties played little part, as the Mensheviks were still supporting the war and the Bolsheviks, with their chief figures in exile abroad or in Siberia, could accomplish little. The revolutionary movement was thus largely spontaneous and unexpected, even though it had long been foreseen.

Protopopov is believed to have had a scheme to promote a popular uprising, which would be put down by troops assembled for the purpose. Then, the government could use the disorder as an excuse for inability to pursue the war and for making a separate peace. Certainly he acted recklessly, for early in 1917 he had the workers' delegation of the War Industry Committee arrested, even though they had been loyal in support of the war. This act did not produce an explosion, however, and merely heightened the tension.

The Uprising. The insurrection began almost un-noticed. Early in March, 1917, a strike of workers of Petrograd's great Putilov Works turned thousands of men onto the streets, to demonstrate against the government and to appeal to the workers of other plants. March 8, International Woman's Day, regularly celebrated by the workers, brought thousands of women from the breadlines to swell the crowds. Red flags and banners with the slogan "Down with the Autocracy!" made their appearance. The police, however, had no great trouble in dispersing the crowds, and the unrest seemed no greater than on previous occasions. By the 9th there were nearly 200,-000 strikers in the streets, demonstrating in the center of the city. Cossacks called out to disperse the crowds refused to charge them, and on one occasion they bowed to the crowd which applauded their inactivity. But the unrest apparently still was not threatening: the British ambassador cabled London: "Some disorders occurred today, but nothing serious."

On March 10 the movement grew in intensity, and the Tsar wired General Khabalov, commander of the garrison, to disperse the crowds with rifle fire. The next day preparations were made to subdue the demonstrations. Police with machine guns were placed in the upper stories of buildings overlooking main thoroughfares, and regiments of the garrison fired with considerable effect on crowds in several parts of the city. The government seemed to have won. But that night the troops in their barracks decided not to shoot down the crowds in the future. When ordered to march on the morning of the 12th, one of the regiments refused, shot the commander, and poured into the streets to join the crowds. Other regiments were quickly won over to the revolution. Together with the workers they hunted down the police and broke into the arsenals, where 40,000 rifles were captured and distributed to the workers. While these events were occurring, M. V. Rodzianko, President of the Duma, wired the Tsar, warning him of the seriousness of the situation and urging immediate reforms to avert a catastrophe. Nicholas said impatiently to his Court Chamberlain: "That fat Rodzianko has written me some nonsense, to which I shall not even reply."

Victory of the Revolution. By nightfall of March 12 it was all over. As the revolution surged ahead, General

Khabalov sought to bring into play his special reserve of troops, but found himself able to collect no more than six companies. This force was sent to drive back the victorious crowds, but on contact with the insurrectionists they melted away, the men going over to the crowds, and the officers into hiding. Finally, late in the day, Khabalov, with less than two thousand men, took refuge in the Winter Palace, only to be asked to leave by the Grand Duke Michael. They went to the nearby Admiralty building, to disperse completely on the following day. The revolution was in full control of Petrograd. The overturn was marked by few excesses and by light casualties. Aside from burning the police stations and hunting down the police, the crowds shed little blood. In all, 1,315 persons, chiefly soldiers and citizens, were killed or wounded.

In the rest of the vast Russian Empire, the revolution spread rapidly, with little fighting. By noon on March 14 the Governor-General of Moscow wired to Headquarters: "In Moscow there is complete insurrection. The military units pass over to the side of the revolutionaries." At the naval bases of Kronstadt and Helsingfors, where hatred of officers was intense, the sailors threw some of them overboard or beat them to death. But these latter actions were exceptional.

The Tsar, at Headquarters, had consistently underestimated the seriousness of the uprising, so that measures to suppress it were taken too late. Only on March 12 did he send a picked force under General Ivanov to pacify the capital. The general expected an easy victory, accomplished by a mere show of force. Before moving, he sent his adjutant out to buy gifts to take to friends in Petrograd, and little effort was made to obtain more troops from other parts of the army. Ivanov's forces, however, failed to reach the capital, as when they came into contact with troops of the suburban garrisons they also went over to the revolution. In all Russia there was no effective defense of the Tsar.

The Revolutionary Government. The Duma was in session when the disorders began, but on March 12 they were prorogued by order of the Tsar, prepared well in advance. The deputies hesitated whether to obey the order of dismissal, but after some thought they accepted it, lest they give aid and comfort to the revolutionaries. They moved from their official meeting place to a room across the hall, where they organized as an unofficial committee with the purpose "of restoring order and to deal with institutions and individuals." In the meantime, as early as March 9, some of the revolutionary leaders, with memories of 1905, suggested the election of a Soviet of Workers' Deputies, and several of factories did hold elections. It was only on March 12, however, that the Soviet assembled in the Tavrida Palace, across the hall from the meeting of the Duma committee. (*See Reading No. 4.*) After it had been joined by delegates from the garrison regiments, it changed its name to Soviet of Workers' and Soldiers' Deputies. Both the Soviet and the Duma were visited by hordes of workers and soldiers, who looked to them for leadership. The Soviet busied itself with the practical matters of the moment—patrolling the streets, feeding the soldiers who had joined the revolution, and similar matters, while the Duma leaders sought to preserve an effective government for the country.

Most of the Duma leaders were convinced monarchists, who felt that a Tsar was essential, even though the abdication of Nicholas II could not be avoided. So it was decided to send a delegation to the Tsar to ask him to abdicate, naming his brother Michael as regent. With some difficulty two of them made their way to the Tsar, who had come part way back to the capital. Before they arrived, Nicholas had heard from all the leading generals that his abdication was essential, so when the delegates appeared he surprised them by readily abdicating in favor of Michael. Back in Petrograd, however, the Duma leaders found it impossible to persuade the masses to accept *any* Tsar and barely escaped violence when they came out for Michael. Nevertheless, on March 16 a group of the Duma leaders, headed by Miliukov, visited Michael to urge him to take the throne. The Grand Duke, however, realizing the public hostility to a monarchy, refused to take the crown except from a Constituent Assembly. Hence, Russia became a republic *de facto*, although the formal declaration of the republic came much later.

Formation of the Provisional Government. The members of the Duma committee felt that they had no right to form a government, but as they realized that if they did not, the leaders of the Soviet, more radical in their outlook, would do so, they decided to take power, "otherwise others will take it, those who have already elected some scoundrels in the factories." Miliukov, especially, sought to establish the authority of the new government by negotiating with the leaders of the Soviet. The latter, however, did not desire to rule, as they were men inexperienced in governmental affairs. Moreover, they were moderate socialists, who believed that at this moment the revolution was bourgeois in character, as the workers were too weak to set up the dictatorship of the proletariat. Hence, the Soviet chiefs felt that power should be entrusted to the leaders of the bourgeoisie, drawn from the ranks of the Duma.

Consequently, on March 14, the leaders of the Duma and the Soviet conferred about the powers and program of the new government, which took office on March 16. The Premier of the Provisional Government was Prince G. E. Lvov, a noted liberal; Guchkov was Minister of War, and Miliukov was Foreign Minister. Alexander Kerensky took the post of Minister of Justice. He was nominally a right-wing Socialist Revolutionary, although he was basically conservative. But his enthusiasm for the revolutionary overturn and his inspiring speeches had made him a popular hero and had won him election to the Soviet. He joined the Provisional Government while retaining his membership in the Soviet for the purpose of serving as a link between the two bodies.

The program of the new regime (*see Reading No. 5*), approved by the Soviet, provided for a full amnesty, broad civil liberties, and complete legal equality of all. Trade unions and strikes were declared legal. The manifesto promised immediate preparation for a constituent assembly, to be elected by universal, direct, equal, and secret voting. Local government was also to be elected. Finally, the soldiers were promised full civil rights, upon condition that firm discipline was observed. This program, which was necessarily a compromise between the Duma and the Soviet, said nothing about the vital issues: the war, and the distribution of land to the peasants. On these points no agreement was possible.

Like its program, the government itself was an uneasy compromise between the Soviet and the leaders of the former Duma. The latter, drawn from the middle-class parties, were quite conservative and instinctively distrusted the masses and the Soviet which represented them. For its part, the Soviet had no great confidence in the Provisional Government. Backed as it was by the vast majority of the workers and the soldiers of the Petrograd garrison, the Soviet undertook to support the Provisional Government only as long as the latter remained true to the cause of the revolution. It compelled the government to arrest the Tsar.

Order No. 1. One of the first acts of the Soviet was to issue its famous Order No. 1 to the troops, to ensure that they would not be used for counter-revolutionary purposes. It was drawn up on March 14 at the suggestion of some of the soldiers. It provided for the election of committees of soldiers in all army units, which were to obey the Soviet and were to keep control of the arms, which were not to be turned over to the officers. The troops were to obey their officers and the Provisional Government, but only insofar as their orders were not in conflict with those of the Soviet. Saluting off duty and elaborate honors to officers were abolished, and the officers were forbidden to be harsh toward their men. These instructions were in part a symptom of the distrust of the officers felt by the rank and file, who had seen that their officers had given no support to the revolution. Discipline in the army had begun to crumble well before the fall of the Tsar. Nevertheless, Order No. 1 doubtless contributed much to the further collapse of the authority of the commanders and of the discipline essential to any effective body of troops. Thus, the Provisional Government lacked effective military support and was dependent for its authority upon the backing of the Soviet.

An Era of Good Feeling. Although in the first weeks after the fall of the monarchy the dualism or divided control of the state held latent the seeds of conflict, matters for a time went fairly smoothly. The Soviet, which grew to over three thousand members, was dominated largely by the soldier delegates, who were usually non-commissioned officers, company clerks, or other partly educated persons, who were not especially radical in their views. Most of them were under the influence of the Socialist Revolutionaries, who supported the war and were not eager for further radicalism. For the most part the workers were led by the Mensheviks, who also supported the war. The latter were convinced that Russia was by no means ready for a proletarian dictatorship, so they were quite ready to let the upper classes represented by the Provisional Government run the country. Even the Bolsheviks did not take an extreme stand at this time.

Kamenev and Stalin, who returned from Siberia during these early days, in their *Pravda* editorials held that, while the war was imperialist in nature, until a general peace became possible there should be no attempt to make a separate peace, and the Russian army should continue to defend the country. And, indeed, even if the Bolsheviks *had* been inspired by the radical views of Lenin, who was fretting in exile in Switzerland, they were too few in numbers and too weak in influence to disturb the relative calm.

Indeed, for a time there was some likelihood that the soldiers might turn against the workers and undo the revolution. The press, chiefly conservative in character, printed many articles insinuating that the workers, by insisting on the eight hour day, were curtailing the output of munitions on which depended the lives of the soldiers, who faced death in the trenches night and day. Groups of soldiers frequently came from the front breathing threats against the slackers in the factories, and it was only thanks to the energetic educational work of the Soviets that the soldiers were gradually persuaded that any shortage of ammunition was caused, not by the selfishness of the workers, but by other factors. Thus the harmony between soldiers and workers was preserved, albeit with some difficulty.

The Moderate Attitude of the Masses. In general, the army, although it had long since lost any enthusiasm for the war, still thought along traditional lines of its duty to defend the country. The general public was thoroughly convinced that the war was an unjust, imperialistic conflict, but the soldiers, although reluctant to respect the authority of their officers, had not begun to demand a separate peace. Desertions were increasingly frequent, but in other respects the army still appeared to be a substantial fighting force. As for the peasants, at first they were quiet. Most of their young, able-bodied men were away in the army, and the old and the very young were not disposed to resort to violence against the landowners. For one thing, the peasants were probably less affected by the economic dislocations of war than most other classes, and, aside from the vast losses of manpower, their lot was not grievous at this time. The Provisional Government, while expressing sympathy with the desire of the peasants to obtain the land, warned the peasants not to take the law into their own hands, but to wait for the Constituent Assembly, which would have full power to decide the matter.

As early as March, 1917, the peasants began to call for peasant Soviets to consider the land question. (*See Reading No. 6.*) Nevertheless, they still remembered their punishment in 1906 and 1907 too well to act rashly, and for a time they were willing to wait. The workers, who had immediately gained the eight hour day as a result of the revolution, also were not yet ready for further insurrection. In March, 1917, factory committees, elected by the workers, were set up, to represent the workers in negotiating with the employers. Although there was much friction between committees and employers, in the early spring the committees were seeking higher wages for the employees rather than confiscation of the factories. As yet the moderate socialists had not been replaced by the militant Bolsheviks who later dominated the committees, and the workers were not in a revolutionary frame of mind.

The Rising Conflict Over Foreign Policy.   At first the Provisional Government took the position that the revolution had changed nothing in Russia's foreign policy. Miliukov, the Foreign Minister, hastened to assure the Allies that Russia stood by her treaty obligations and warmed their hearts by stating that the Tsar had been overthrown because his government had not been able to wage war with sufficient energy—a far from correct statement. Miliukov was especially interested in obtaining Constantinople and the Dardanelles for Russia, which had been promised by the secret treaties of 1915. The moderate socialists who dominated the Soviet, however, felt that the war was essentially imperialistic in character and hoped that the peoples of the other warring states would also overturn their governments and demand peace.

With this end in view, on March 27 the Soviet issued a

"Manifesto to the Peoples of the World," calling on them to oppose actively the annexationist policies of their governments. (*See Reading No. 7.*) The Russian democracy, the manifesto promised, would resist to the death all efforts of its ruling classes to pursue such a policy. The peoples of the West, especially in Germany, should rise in revolution against kings, landowners, and bankers, and thus bring about a revolutionary peace. But until this should happen, the Soviet declared, the Russian revolution would not retreat before conquering bayonets nor allow itself to be crushed by outside force. This manifesto was widely hailed by the socialist press, which strongly demanded a peace "without annexations and indemnities."

Miliukov, however, did not share this attitude. Early in April he issued a press interview stating that Russia was fighting to unite the Ukrainian parts of the Austro-Hungarian Empire with Russia and to gain Constantinople and the Straits. These objectives, he declared, could not be regarded as annexation. This utterance aroused a storm of protest. Conflict was averted, however, when the Provisional Government published a "Declaration on War Aims" renouncing annexations and upholding self-determination. It added, however, that Russia should not "emerge from the great struggle humiliated, undermined in her vital strength." The Provisional Government stated its determination "to protect national rights while strictly fulfilling the obligations assumed toward the Allies." In these vague phrases Miliukov saw support for his design to win Constantinople.

Lenin's Return. The news of the fall of the monarchy and the forming of the Provisional Government found Lenin in Switzerland, where he had spent much of the war years. During this period he had formulated his attitude toward the war. Capitalism, he held, must inevitably lead to imperialism, and imperialism is bound to produce war for the interests of the capitalists. In such a conflict the working class had no interest, but should strive to transform the war into a civil war. The socialists of Europe who had supported their nation's cause after Serajevo were thus traitors to the proletariat. Only a true Marxist party could be trusted to end the war in the interests of the working class.

Holding these views, Lenin was frantically eager to return to Russia, but found that no Allied country would permit him to cross its territory. He was thus bottled up in Switzerland. In his despair he even hoped to pass in disguise as a Swede, with the help of a forged Swedish passport, covering his ignorance of the language by pretending to be dumb. Fortunately for him, this proved not to be necessary. Swiss socialist leaders arranged with the German government to let him and a number of other Russian exiles travel across Germany in a sealed car to Denmark; from there he made his way to Sweden and Finland, and on April 16 he reached Petrograd. Although he had expected to be arrested by the Provisional Government, to his surprise he was met by a deputation from the Soviet and a guard of honor at the Finland Station. He impatiently turned from his official welcome to address the throngs of people in a fiery speech ending with the words: "Long live the socialist revolution!"

The April Theses. On April 17, the day after his arrival, Lenin presented his revolutionary program to two gatherings: one of Bolsheviks, and the second of Bolsheviks and Mensheviks together. The program, known as the April Theses (*see Reading No. 8*), contained ten points. It declared that the war was still an imperialistic one, to be ended by the overthrow of capitalism and fraternization of the soldiers with the enemy. The revolution, he held, should immediately take the power from the hands of the bourgeoisie and give it to the proletariat and poorer peasants. No support should be given to the Provisional Government, which should be replaced by the Soviet of Workers' Deputies. All large estates were to be nationalized and turned over to the Soviets of Farmhands' Deputies.

This program, in particular as it concerned the war, horrified even the Bolshevik leaders, who felt that it was utterly unrealistic. The Mensheviks regarded Lenin as so visionary as to be ludicrous and felt joy at his impracticability. His program was promptly rejected by the Bolsheviks, 12 to 2, and *Pravda* wrote that his proposals were based upon an incorrect analysis of the revolution. But Lenin was not dismayed by this reception. He pushed his program in incessant speeches to streams of men and women who came to hear him, and so simple and so logical did his points of "End the war" and "All land to the peasants" seem that he won their complete support. His propaganda enjoyed such success among the masses that his party swung over to his side, and at an All-Russian Conference of Bolsheviks in May it strongly approved the program that it had rejected three weeks before. Thus, the lines began to form for a struggle between the Provisional Government and the masses, urged on by Lenin.

— 5 —

THE MOUNTING CRISIS

The Fall of Miliukov. Miliukov's trickery in attempting to cover his annexationist aims with vague words soon came out into the open. When it was discovered that the Allies had not heard of the "Declaration of War Aims," there was a strong demand that he communicate it officially to them. He did so on May 1, but accompanied the Declaration with a covering note (*see Reading No. 9*), in which he affirmed that Russia was determined to carry the war "to a decisive conclusion," in order to obtain "sanctions and guarantees" which would make new wars impossible. ("Sanctions and guarantees" sounded ominously like annexations.) Finally, he again promised to "fulfill Russia's obligations to her Allies." When, on May 3, this note became public, it was taken as a deliberate challenge to the wishes of the public. (*See Reading No. 10.*) The people felt that their strivings for peace had been nullified by the obstinate Foreign Minister.

A crisis of extreme seriousness resulted, with mass demonstrations in front of the seat of the Provisional Government. Although some of the demonstrators supported Miliukov, most of them, including fully armed regiments, carried banners demanding peace without annexations and indemnities, the end of the war, and the dismissal of Miliukov. On the next day, there were even stronger demonstrations, in which there were demands for the end of the Provisional Government. General L. G. Kornilov, commander of the Petrograd garrison, wanted to use his troops to smash the demonstration, but severe bloodshed was averted by the Petrograd Soviet, which ordered that no regiment should come out into the streets without an order signed by the Soviet. Kornilov, angered by this check upon his authority, resigned his command and went to the front.

The demonstration was quickly checked by the orders of the Soviet. The Provisional Government hastened to calm the public by issuing its explanation of Miliukov's note, which it sent to the Allied ambassadors. It practically disavowed Miliukov's interpretation and repeated the pacifist phrases of the earlier declarations. As Miliukov held to his views (*see Reading No. 11*), he now had to give up the Foreign Ministry, and he refused a lesser post. Likewise Guchkov, Minister of War, also resigned, in part because of poor health, and partly from despair with the trend of events. These resignations led to a reorganization of the Provisional Government, which reformed with nine ministers from the former Duma (chiefly Cadets), and six moderate socialists from the Soviet. It was hoped that this coalition would end the friction between the Soviet and the Provisional Government. The result, however, was to transfer the disharmony into the midst of the government itself. Probably the chief figure in the new regime was Kerensky, the Minister of War.

This crisis clearly showed the growing radicalism of the Petrograd populace and the rising influence of the Bolsheviks. They continued to grow in prestige, thanks to Lenin's untiring efforts and to the arrival of Trotsky. This brilliant, somewhat erratic figure, who had been living in New York when the Tsar fell, had been stopped by the British while *en route* to Russia and held at Halifax. With some difficulty British socialists secured his release. On his arrival, Trotsky, nominally a Menshevik, threw in his fortune with Lenin and the Bolsheviks in opposition to the war and the Provisional Government. His passionate, convincing oratory did much to win the soldiers and the workers to the Bolsheviks and away from the government. (Stalin was also active throughout this period, but in a less noteworthy fashion. One keen observer later wrote that at this time Stalin seemed to be only "a gray blur.")

The Lull Before the Storm. The Provisional Government, and especially the Cadet party, which was rapidly absorbing the other conservative parties, seemed little concerned over the rise of the Bolsheviks. The chief hope of the conservatives was the coming offensive of the army, which through its victories was to restore military discipline and preserve the country from anarchy, as well as to bring closer the end of the war. In spite of pessimistic warnings from Generals Alexeev and Lukomsky, Kerensky was sure of victory and threw himself into the work of preparing for the offensive. (*See Reading No. 12.*) Special "shock battalions" or "battalions of death," including some composed of women, were formed, in hopes that they would give an inspiring example. Above all, Kerensky relied upon persuasion, making emotional, enthusiastic speeches with all his nervous energy. To his great encouragement, he was usually warmly applauded by the men, who swore to do their duty to the fatherland and the revolution. After he had gone, however, the war-weariness of the men again aserted itself and the officers could exert no more authority than before.

In Petrograd, also, the situation seemed good. The Bolsheviks, while growing, remained a considerable minority, while the moderate socialists remained in control of the Soviet. But here, too, the reality was not reassuring to the moderates. While the masses out of habit voted for socialists, at the same time they often would vote for Bolshevik resolutions. Nevertheless, when the First Congress of Soviets met on June 16, 1917, the Bolsheviks and allied groups had only 137 out of the 1,090 members. Tseretelli, a moderate leader of the Petrograd Soviet, was sufficiently encouraged by the lack of Bolshevik strength to declare in his speech (*see Reading No. 13*) that the government was secure, "as there is no political party in Russia which at the present time would say: 'Give us power.'" But at this point Lenin spoke from his seat: "Yes, there is!"

The First Threat to the Provisional Government.
Lenin's unexpected remark was the first sign that a crisis
was at hand. He made it even more plain in his speech
a little later, startling the Congress by blaming all the
country's ills on the greed of the bourgeoisie, which should
be cured by arresting fifty or one hundred of their number. He declared that the Bolsheviks should take power,
as the war could be ended only by pushing the revolution
to new lengths. He flatly rejected the support given by
England and France. "Let the Russian revolutionary
classes say: 'Down with this support; I do not recognize
the debts contracted with the British and French capitalists; I appeal for a rising of all against the capitalists!' "

The Congress of Soviets took little notice of Lenin's
speech and voted a series of resolutions calling for support of the Provisional Government. (*See Reading No.
14.*) None the less, the soldiers and the workers of Petrograd, who were thoroughly aroused, insisted on demonstrating against the government. The Bolsheviks, with
reluctance, agreed to lead the demonstration, which was,
however, called off by the Congress of Soviets on June 24.
Later, the Congress called for a demonstration to show
that the revolutionary front was still strong. On July 1
some three or four hundred thousand soldiers and workers turned out for the demonstration, which, however,
was completely dominated by the Bolsheviks. The banners bore slogans: "An End to the War!" "Down with
the Ten Capitalist Ministers!" that boded no good to the
government. Nevertheless, the demonstration ended peace-
fully.

Other Difficulties of the Government.   The government was also faced with other troubles. On June 24 a
Ukrainian Military Congress, led by Ukrainian Nationalists, issued a "Universal Act" insisting that all Ukrainian
military units should take orders from the new Ukrainian
Rada (Council), which on June 28 set up its General
Secretariat to act as the executive organ for the Ukraine.
The Soviet of Kronstadt, the naval base near Petrograd,
led by highly radical elements, practically refused to recognize the authority of the Provisional Government.
Moreover, within the government itself there were dis-
sensions. On July 1 the Minister of Commerce and Industry resigned after a disagreement with the socialist

Minister of Labor, and in mid-July four Cadet Ministers resigned in protest against concessions to the Ukrainians. Thus, when the climax of revolutionary disturbance was reached in the July Days (July 16-18, 1917), the government was in a gravely weakened condition.

The Military Debacle.   On July 1, 1917, the Russian offensive began in Galicia. (*See Reading No. 15.*) The Russians, with great superiority in numbers and thanks to an unprecedented artillery preparation, penetrated the Austrian lines at several points near Lvov and took several thousand prisoners. Soon, however, they encountered unexpected resistance. The attack, which on other fronts had had no success, bogged down after twelve days. On July 19, the Germans and Austrians began a counter-drive which met almost no opposition as the Russians fled headlong. (*See Reading No. 16.*) All discipline vanished and the rout intensified, accompanied by terrible outrages inflicted on the civilians as the troops fled. Finally the line stabilized after all Galicia had been given up; but it was the decision of the enemy rather than Russian resistance that ended the retreat. General Kornilov, who was appointed to command the Southwest Front on July 20, demanded the death penalty in the front areas, and immediately used machine guns and artillery on masses of deserters and mutineers. On July 25, the Provisional Government restored the death penalty and set up special military tribunals to deal with major offenses. But not even these measures accomplished much, for the morale of the army was ruined beyond repair.

The July Insurrection.   While the Russian offensive was continuing, violence erupted in Petrograd. The masses of workers, already very hostile toward the Provisional Government, and the soldiers of the garrison, fearful that they might be sent to the front, grew impatient with the apparent timidity of the Bolshevik leadership. On July 16 the First Machine Gun Regiment, an especially radical unit, marched forth, although both the Soviets (*see Reading No. 17*) and the Bolsheviks sought to restrain them. The revolutionary call of the soldiers was eagerly obeyed by other troop units and by hundreds of thousands of workers, whom the Bolsheviks reluctantly led, in order to keep them from getting completely out of hand. On July 17, perhaps 500,000 in huge columns poured through the streets with banners demanding "All Power to the Soviets!" and "Down with the Provisional Government!" They converged on the Tavrida Palace, seat of the Central Executive Committee of the Soviets, to demand that this body assume power in place of the Provisional Government. Feelings ran extremely high, as the demonstrators, augmented by a large force of fierce sailors from Kronstadt, armed to the teeth, streamed through the streets. Occasional shots were fired, at which the demonstrators, believing themselves under attack from neighboring buildings, broke into the houses to hunt for snipers. Several score of persons were killed, and over one hundred wounded. Some of the ministers had narrow escapes. Kerensky was almost captured on the first day, and Victor Chernov, the socialist Minister of Agriculture, escaped death at the hands of sailors only through the intervention of Trotsky.

In the meantime, in the palace, the Central Executive Committee, composed chiefly of Mensheviks and Socialist Revolutionaries, was beset by masses of furious armed men who demanded that they take power—something they refused to do. (*See Reading No. 18.*) A stalemate developed as frustrated soldiers and workers threatened the frightened but stubborn leaders of the Soviet to induce them to take power. But the long discussions proved fruitless, and the Bolsheviks, who could easily have seized all Petrograd by giving the order, failed to do so, so that eventually the demonstrators grew weary and went home. The sailors boarded their ships and went back to Kronstadt, and the Central Executive Commitee could breathe more freely.

Reaction Against Lenin and the Bolsheviks. The tide of revolt receded as quickly as it had risen. Several of the Guards regiments, which had not taken part in the demonstration, were informed on July 17 that the Minister of Justice had documentary proof that Lenin was a German agent. The Guards, convinced by this, at once put themselves at the orders of the government and the Central Executive Committee. The danger was now over, and on the following day government forces raided and wrecked the offices and plant of *Pravda* and occupied without a struggle the Fortress of Peter and Paul and the

Bolshevik headquarters. On July 19 a Bolshevik leaflet announced that the demonstration was at an end.

The documents charging Lenin and other Bolshevik leaders with treason were published in the newspapers, much to the annoyance of Kerensky, who claimed that this had prevented Lenin's capture and punishment. Other ministers were very dubious about the documents and their source. The middle classes, however, were easily convinced of the correctness of the charges, as they remembered that Lenin had left Switzerland in a German train. Warrants were issued for his arrest, and also for Zinoviev and Kamenev. Both Lenin and Zinoviev hid, although they protested their innocence. Lenin at first wanted to stand trial, but as he was persuaded by his associates that he might be murdered in prison, he escaped to Finland, where the Russian police could not follow. He stayed in Helsingfors until autumn. Trotsky and several other Bolsheviks were arrested, but were soon released.

It is perhaps worth stating that most historians of repute do not believe that Lenin was a German agent, even though the Germans had enabled him to return to Russia. Lenin was a fanatical revolutionary, to whom money meant little. If, for purposes of its own, the Imperial German Government would help him, he, for his own purposes was ready to accept. He did what the Germans had expected he would, which is what they wanted. But he did it because he wanted to, not to please them.

Government Policy After the July Days. The Provisional Government took advantage of its improved position to take further action. Legislation was adopted against incitement to mutiny. Regiments that had taken the lead in the uprising were disbanded and the men sent to the front, in some cases with the use of force. Several of the Bolshevik newspapers were closed and circulation of such publications among the troops was forbidden. At the same time, General Kornilov was demanding the death penalty at the front and was applying severe measures of discipline. These actions were strongly endorsed by conservative organizations, both civilian and military, which hopefully discerned a trend to the Right. A vague feeling of counter-revolution was in the air and was noted with concern by moderate socialists of the Soviets and the trade unions. Some of these bodies in dismay passed resolutions condemning the government's policies and exonerating the Bolsheviks. As for the masses of soldiers and workers, they seem to have wavered but little in their belief in Lenin, although they were compelled to relapse into sullen inactivity.

The moderate and the conservative elements of Russia had been granted a new lease of life by the unexpected outcome of the July Days. Neither group, however, took advantage of the opportunity to satisfy the enormous popular demand for peace and land, which was the basis of the strength of the Bolsheviks. The moderate Left continued to advocate prosecution of the war to victory and urged that the land and other problems be deferred until the Constituent Assembly, which, it must be said, they did little to hasten. Thus, they did nothing of significance to win the masses from the Bolsheviks and, hence, remained without any real popular following. As for the Right—landowners, capitalists, army officers, and other upper-class elements—they had never accepted the revolutionary regime in their hearts, and now that the rabble had been subdued, they felt that they discerned the delightful possibility of a strong man—a military dictatorship—to sweep aside all this rubbish of socialists and soviets and to establish sound law and order again, as before the revolution.

— 6 —

THE KORNILOV MOVEMENT

The Illusion of Calm. Although the collapse of the July demonstration had apparently ended all danger from the Bolsheviks, the improvement in the government's position was largely on the surface, while underneath the situation grew worse. On instructions from Lenin, the Bolsheviks concentrated their efforts on the factory committees, which were becoming more and more aggressive. The factory workers found that the rapid inflation raised prices far more than they could raise their wages, and the poorer paid were especially hard hit. The declaration of the textile workers that their children were dying like flies as a result of hunger was not entirely rhetoric. Hence, the lot of the workers became unbearable and they turned to the factory committees for redress and to the Bolsheviks for leadership.

More and more the workers came under Bolshevik influence, which was reflected in stiffer demands upon their employers. The latter, however, pleaded that the higher costs and the shortage of fuel and raw materials made their position impossible, and in some instances factories were shut down, thereby making the workers more desperate than ever. Already in midsummer there were cases where workers took over idle factories and tried to run them, claiming that the closing was sabotage by the employers. Although the Red Guards—the armed bands of workers that were formed early in the revolution—were largely disarmed after the July Days, the workingmen were in a more belligerent frame of mind than ever.

The peasants, also, were becoming rebellious. During the summer they became more and more impatient with the government's advice to wait until the Constituent Assembly for agrarian legislation, especially after that body had been postponed until November. The peasants could see that the Land Committees functioning under Chernov, the Minister of Agriculture, were doing little to help them. The Bolsheviks had little contact with the peasants, while their traditional leaders, the Socialist Revolutionaries, were badly split. The rank and file of this party encouraged the peasants to take action, thus showing that they were closer to the revolutionary policy of the Bolsheviks than to the conservative and restraining policy of nominal Socialist Revolutionaries like Kerensky and other leaders. The peasants needed little urging to make them active. Although they rarely attacked the estates of the nobility, they encroached more and more upon their holdings and made their farming operations difficult. The government uttered pleading appeals and rebukes, but the peasants, meeting little or no repression, grew ever bolder, while the landowners were increasingly desperate.

To add to the woes of the government, the national minorities became increasingly self-assertive. As Poland and most of the Baltic states were held by the Germans, they were not an active problem; but both Finland and the Ukraine were becoming restless. In July, the Finnish Diet introduced a bill that virtually proclaimed Finnish independence, and, although the Provisional Government vetoed it as unconstitutional, the Finns continued to push the measure. As for the Ukrainians, the *Rada* in Kiev claimed that it spoke for the whole nation, and Ukrainian regiments recognized its authority. There is reason to believe, however, that the nationalists were by no means strong, as even in Kiev the Soviet exercised control, while in Kharkov and the eastern Ukraine the nationalist movement amounted to little. Nevertheless, the Ukrainians as well as the Finns were numbered among the Provisional Government's problems.

The Kerensky Government. The coalition formed after the July Days failed to endure, for on July 21 Prince Lvov resigned his post as Premier in disapproval of the socialist policy of Chernov, Minister of Agriculture, and others. Kerensky thereupon took office as Premier. After much negotiating and scheming a new government was installed in early August, with eleven socialists and seven nonsocialists. In spite of the preponderance of socialists, however, the new government was more conservative than its predecesor, as the socialists, frightened by the events of July, had lost all trace of revolutionary zeal. More and more, Kerensky dominated the scene. While he still commanded a liberal following, he was no radical, but rather wished to leave the social order undisturbed. Thus, although his government had a majority of nominal socialists, in revolutionary parlance it was "bourgeois," as its policies were closer to those of the propertied classes than to the program of the leaders of the proletariat. To the increasingly embittered masses of Petrograd, it probably seemed ominous that in August Kerensky took up residence in the Winter Palace, the abode of the Tsars.

Weakness of the Kerensky Regime. The chief weakness of Kerensky's government was that it was not backed by an assembly that really represented the people. The Central Executive Committee, composed of Mensheviks and Socialist Revolutionaries, for the most part supported the government, as it had no real reason to oppose it and, moreover, could see no alternative to it. But the Central Executive Committee was losing its claim to represent the masses. The July Days had shown how strong the opposition to it was in Petrograd. By mid-August the Workers' Section of the Petrograd Soviet had come under Bolshevik leadership, and not long afterward the second Conference of Factory Committees met, under Bolshevik control. But, although Kerenesky probably sensed the weakness of the foundation of his government, he found it impossible to summon the Constituent Assembly before November.

Kerensky resorted to what proved to be an unreliable substitute. A State Conference was summoned to meet in Moscow late in August, in hopes that it would demonstrate the unity of the Russians in support of their government. But it, also, was not representative. This gathering of nearly 2,500 members consisted of deputies from various institutions throughout the country: the four Dumas, the Soviets, the local governments, cooperative societies, trade unions, universities, the army, and the liberal professions. The associations of landowners and manufacturers were also represented. The Bolsheviks were not present. The Moscow State Conference included most of the famous people of Russia, and their support was expected to lend great prestige to the Provisional Government.

The Rise of General Kornilov.   One of the most prominent members of the Conference was General L. G. Kornilov, the new commander-in-chief. He was a dashing soldier who had won great fame by his exploits in the war as well as by his spectacular personality. A Siberian, with somewhat Mongolian features, he was followed with devotion by a bodyguard of wild Caucasian cavalrymen, whose language he knew. In May, as commander of the Petrograd garrison, he had wished to smash the demonstration against Miliukov, and when the Soviet had prevented this he had resigned to go to the front. Kornilov's reputation as a Napoleonic figure had been further enhanced by his ruthless measures in dealing with the routed troops after the disastrous July offensive. He was greatly admired by Boris Savinkov, the former Socialist Revolutionary who had become head of the Ministry of War under Kerensky, and as Kerensky felt that Kornilov would be successful in reviving the fighting spirit of the army, the general had been named commander-in-chief on July 31. Kornilov's conditions for taking over this post, amounting to a virtual free hand with the army, as well as the extension of full military control to the rear military areas, indicated that he would be a difficult person to handle. The friction caused by this stand was soon eliminated when Kornilov agreed to a compromise, but the incident gave a hint of trouble to come.

Kornilov's Dictatorial Tendencies. Kornilov, who had little knowledge of politics, soon became a storm center. He was instinctively hostile to all socialists, whether extreme or mild, and he disliked Kerensky, although he promised to work with him. The Leftist press, which saw in him a danger to the revolution, attacked him strongly, asking that he be replaced by a general more in sympathy with the revolutionary cause. Conservatives and reactionaries became his enthusiastic allies. The Union of Cossack Troops warned that the consequences for the army would be disastrous if he were removed—an opinion voiced by other military organizations. The conservatives of Moscow, headed by M. V. Rodzianko, former chairman of the Duma, wired him: "In this threatening hour of severe trial all thinking Russia looks to you with hope and faith." Kornilov was greatly pleased by these proofs of strong support, not realizing that they came from a relatively few persons who had no popular backing.

As early as August 19 or 20, 1917, Kornilov ordered a corps of Cossacks and the Wild Division of Caucasians to concentrate within striking distance of Petrograd, ostensibly to protect the government. But when, at a meeting with the Premier on August 23, Kornilov's proposal for military rule on the railways and in war industries was adopted only in very diluted form, Kornilov told his chief of staff: "It's time to hang the German supporters and spies, with Lenin at their head, and to disperse the Soviet of Workers' and Soldiers' Deputies so that it will never reassemble." He added that he was planning to send the cavalry to Petrograd under General Krymov, who, if need arose, would hang every member of the Soviet.

The Moscow State Conference. Kornilov's *coup
d'état* was already taking shape by August 25. It gained
even greater momentum as a result of the Moscow State
Conference, which took place on August 25-28. Ironi-
cally enough, this meeting, whose purpose was to demonstrate the unity of all behind the government, met in a
Moscow without streetcars and without lights; even the
restaurants were not functioning, thanks to a one-day
general strike called by the Bolsheviks. The Conference,
far from supporting Kerensky's government, turned into
an overt demonstration of the Right, whose hostility toward Kerensky was plain to see. (*See Reading No. 19.*)

Kerensky's opening speech, condemning both Bolshevik
turbulence and a hypothetical Rightist uprising, was
warmly applauded by his supporters of the moderate
Left, but was greeted with stony silence by the Right.
On the second day, when Kornilov arrived, he was met
by a guard of honor, bands playing, and loud cheers. Various Rightist organizations gave him an enthusiastic greet-
ing, and amid loud hurrahs he was showered with flowers.
When Kornilov spoke he disappointed his admirers by not
giving a call to arms, but General Kaledin of the Don
Cossacks made up for his mildness. In a fiery speech
Kaledin demanded that "all Soviets and committees must
be abolished, both in the army and in the rear." This met
with strong approval from the Right, but the Left greeted
it with hisses. Kerensky later made an emotional appeal
for unity in the hour of Russia's trial, but he failed to restore harmony, and the widening split was ominous.

The Preliminaries to the Uprising. The outcome
of the Moscow State Conference was to confirm Kornilov
and his supporters in the belief that Kerensky could never
restore order in Russia, for which Kornilov was the essential man. Rodzianko, Miliukov, and other leaders of the
Duma period, energetically enrolled landowners and financial magnates in well financed organizations to further
the cause, while generals and officers built up organizations of officers and military cadets to support the march
on Petrograd by uprisings at the right moment. Kornilov's
chief-of-staff later claimed that there were thousands in
Petrograd waiting to strike in support of the movement.
On September 6, Savinkov, head of the War Ministry un-

der Kerensky, with the latter's approval, visited Kornilov at Headquarters and approved the commander's demands for introducing the death penalty in the rear, Savinkov also told him that as a Bolsheivk uprising was expected within a few days, he should send a cavalry corps to the capital to protect the Provisional Government.

This request, which Kornilov had already anticipated by sending troops, was part of the political scheme to which Savinkov was a party. Kerensky was to be invited to dismiss the government and form a new one in which he, Kornilov, and Savinkov would be the dominant figures. If Kerensky refused, the troops were to be brought into play. Unfortunately for the success of the scheme, V. N. Lvov, a lesser political figure, undertook to persuade Kerensky to cooperate, and thereby gave the Premier warning. Kerensky, realizing that if the scheme went through his freedom, if not his life, would be in danger, at once took steps against the conspiracy. After arresting Lvov, on September 9 he ordered Kornilov to resign and asked for support from the Soviet and from the ministers. The Soviet at once gave him full support, but the Cadet ministers resigned from the government, apparently hoping to cause its collapse.

In addition to the dissension within his cabinet, Kerensky was faced with great pressure to "compromise" the difficulty by resigning in favor of General Alexeev. Miliukov and several of Kerensky's own cabinet urged that he resign in favor of Alexeev, as did great numbers of other conservatives. Sir George Buchanan, the British ambassador, in the name of the diplomatic corps, also urged Kerensky to compromise. For a time he wavered, even going so far as to recall his condemnation of Kornilov, but eventually the break became complete. Indeed, the proposed compromise was no compromise at all, as General Alexeev was one of Kornilov's most ardent supporters, so that Kerensky's resignation would have eased Kornilov's road to power.

The Collapse of the Movement. Undismayed by Kerensky's opposition, Kornilov persisted in his undertaking, issuing a blast against the Provisional Government, charging it with collaborating with the Germans and ruining the army and the country. He appealed to the populace in a manifesto (*see Reading No. 20*) full of national-

ist and religious phrases, which, however, had already lost
their potency. With almost complete support from the
Allies, and even aided by a British unit of armored cars,
whose men had donned Russian uniforms, he was certain
of success. Most of the army leaders were with him, he
was sure of the Wild Division and the Cossacks, and he
counted on the aid of other disciplined troops. The garrison of Petrograd seemed to have no great enthusiasm for
fighting for Kerensky. As for the Petrograd populace, he
felt that they, unorganized and leaderless, would remain in
sullen apathy, "an indifference that submits to the whip."
General Krymov and the other field commanders were
ordered to advance on Petrograd.

As soon as the Soviet in Petrograd realized the approaching danger, it hastened to act. Despairing of Kerensky's leadership, the Soviet leaders threw themselves
into the work of defending the capital. On September 9,
moderate socialists and Bolsheviks combined in a "Committee for Struggle against Counter-Revolution" to defeat
Kornilov. The garrison was put in a state of readiness,
neighboring troops were called to their aid, and large
numbers of eager sailors from Kronstadt arrived, with
more coming from other parts of the fleet. Under Bolshevik leadership the Petrograd workers were mobilized.
Trenches were dug, barbed wire was strung, barricades
were built in the city streets. The Red Guards from the
factories, who had been disarmed after the July Days,
were again given weapons, and turned out, full of fight.
Strong detachments were sent to break up the officers'
organizations that had planned to rise as Krymov's forces
approached. The conspiratorial center in the Hotel
Astoria was taken without difficulty, and a sweeping
series of arrests and searches eliminated other groups of
plotters. A colonel sent by Kornilov to direct the movement fled to Finland. In all, some 7,000 arrests were
made by the Soviet, thus ending all danger of an officers'
uprising in Petrograd.

The Failure of the Troop Movements. Not content
to await the arrival of the attacking forces, the Soviet had
sent word to the railway workers to impede the movement of the hostile troops. At the orders of their union
the men cut telegraph wires, put locomotives out of commission, blocked tracks by tipping over freight cars, tore

up rails. As the troop trains progressed, they were switched off in the wrong direction and finally halted, isolated and helpless. At once the puzzled troops were met by numbers of propagandists sent by the Soviet and by soldiers from nearby garrisons, who explained to the men that there had been no uprising of Bolsheviks against the government in Petrograd. They were being led, they were told, to overthrow the revolutionary government in order that the upper classes might restore the old regime. Even the Wild Division, composed of Caucasian mountaineers, was met by a number of their countrymen sent out by the Soviet, who handed them pamphlets in the chief Caucasian languages and explained the real nature of the expedition. The officers fumed but could do nothing. Finally, the soldiers elected a committee which on September 13 went to Petrograd to apologize to the Soviet for having unwittingly marched against it. The Cossacks fared no better. With their movement by rail blocked and without the supplies for an advance on foot, they were helpless. The Cossacks, too, refused to fight against the Soviet and began to turn against their officers. The campaign was over, with no unit having fired a shot.

General Kornilov, who had remained at Headquarters, ill with a fever, soon found himself completely unable to send reenforcements to the troops advancing on Petrograd, as the railway workers had isolated him from the rest of the country. Even many of the troops on which he had counted turned against him and refused to obey his orders. General A. I. Denikin, commander of the Southwest front, was arrested when he tried to dispatch troops against the capital. Several other generals sent word they would have no part in Kornilov's movement. No troops could be found who were willing to march against the Soviets. Finally, when word came that General Krymov, who led the expedition against the capital, had gone to Petrograd and, after a stormy scene with Kerensky, had shot himself, Kornilov realized that his cause was lost.

The Aftermath of the Kornilov Coup. Kerensky, who had been saved by the spontaneous action of the Soviet and the Bolsheviks, was far from happy about his position after the episode. He now realized that, with the power of the Right destroyed, the Left had gained greatly in strength. Hence, he sought to use the remaining conservatives as a counterweight to the now rising popular forces. To replace Kornilov as commander-in-chief Kerensky named, not one of the generals in sympathy with the revolution, but General Alexeev, who had been hand-in-glove with Kornilov. Moreover, Kerensky ordered that, until Alexeev arrived at Headquarters, the army should continue to obey Kornilov's orders. Alexeev promptly cancelled the movement of strong revolutionary forces to subdue Kornilov's Headquarters garrison. It was only with the greatest reluctance that he had the insurgent general arrested on September 14, along with his most obvious supporters. The arrested men were transferred to a town in the Ukraine, where they were nominally imprisoned. The jailers were none other than Kornilov's devoted Caucasian bodyguard.

An extraordinary investigating committee was sent out to gather evidence against the conspirators, but they showed no willingness to take action and soon released all but the five chief participants. It was obvious that Kerensky's government was not willing to deal harshly with the insurgents. To the masses of soldiers and workers, who had been willing to risk their lives to suppress the Kornilov insurrection, this tenderness toward the defeated generals seemed as treasonable as the uprising itself.

— 7 —

THE AFTERMATH OF THE KORNILOV AFFAIR

Another Chance for Kerensky. After the threat from Kornilov had been removed, Kerensky, although his prestige was badly shaken by his unwillingness to punish the rebels, still had an opportunity to bring the government into line with the aspirations of the people. It is conceivable that if he had accepted reality and had decided to support the demand for peace and had approved a land program satisfactory to the peasants, a more violent revolutionary outbreak could still have been avoided. A moderate democratic regime was perhaps still possible. Instead of making a sharp change in direction, however, the government remained much as before. It still depended on the old Central Executive Committee of the Soviet which had been elected in the earlier, conservative period and which did not represent the feelings of the masses. The Socialist Revolutionaries and the Mensheviks who composed it had been left behind by the rapid march of events. Beneath the surface the Soviets were beginning to swing to the Bolsheviks, while peasants and soldiers were no longer willing to support the war and to wait for a much-postponed Constituent Assembly to deal with the land problem. The appeal of the Right to counter-revolutionary force had made the masses far more impatient with the inaction of the government and more ready to decide the issue by a new resort to the enormous revolutionary force that still remained.

More than ever the government of Russia centered in Kerensky. After the crisis was over, the ministers, who had tendered their resignations, remained in office for a time on a day-to-day basis. On September 14, a Directory or inner cabinet of five men, headed by Kerensky, was set up to determine policy. On the same day, Russia was proclaimed a republic. This step, which merely recognized what had long been obvious, met with strong opposition on the part of the conservatives, who asserted that it exceeded the powers of the Provisional Government. Many felt that beneath the legalistic basis for the protest there lingered a strong hope on the part of the conservatives that somehow the monarchy could be restored.

The New Coalition. As the second coalition government had broken up as a result of the Kornilov uprising, it was necessary to form a new coalition which, it was hoped, would have some popular support. Hence a Democratic Conference was summoned to meet in Petrograd on September 27, 1917. It was composed of delegates from the Soviets, the *zemstvos,* the nationality organizations, the trade unions, the cities, and the co-operatives. The gathering, whose 1,200 members did not include members of the propertied classes, was quite radical in sentiment. At the outset it voted by a small majority to approve the principle of forming a coalition, but proposals to accept Cadets (Constitutional Democrats) and other pro-Kornilov parties were rejected by strong majorities. Nevertheless, a final vote on a proposal to reject coalition with parties of the Right failed to carry, so that there was no clear expression of the wishes of the Conference, although it certainly was not enthusiastic about including the Cadets.

Nevertheless, in spite of the lack of firm support, Kerensky went ahead anyhow, forming a new ministry which included three Cadets. This troubled millions of Russians, who felt that the Cadet party as a whole, by its complicity in the Kornilov affair, had lost its right to share in the government. Kerensky's naming of Cadets to ministerial portfolios suggested that his attitude toward the conspiracy was ambiguous. On the other hand, the appointment of General Alexander Verkhovsky as Minister of War promised well, as he was known to be in sympathy with the aims of the revolution.

Verkhovsky's Program. The appointment of General Alexeev as commander-in-chief quickly produced friction between him and Kerensky, with the result that the latter assumed command of the armies in person, although he had had no military training. For this reason the naming of Verkhovsky as Minister of War was highly important. He had strongly opposed Kornilov and his program and was the one general of importance who had some understanding of the real situation in Russia. He enjoyed the enthusiastic support of the moderate Left for his willingness to adopt a policy in harmony with popular demands. In fact, he even established friendly relations with the Bolsheviks of Moscow, who were moderate in their views, and vainly sought to gain the cooperation of the Petrograd Bolsheviks.

Verkhovsky's attitude toward the war was refreshingly new. He recognized that for Russia there was no hope of victory and that she and the Allies should offer Germany a just, democratic peace. He insisted that the Russians must "compel the Allies to agree to peace negotiations, otherwise this will cause them inestimable harm." If this should prove impossible, Russia should reduce her huge army to a force that could be fed and maintained, even though this would entail assuming a purely defensive policy. If the Germans should attack this smaller army, the Russians should use the traditional maneuver of retreating into the interior, while keeping the army in being and stimulating its revolutionary ardor. Fundamental social reforms, similar to the agrarian reforms sought by Chernov, also figured in Verkhovsky's program. He felt that unless the government could win the enthusiastic support of the masses by looking after their needs, both in industry and in agriculture, there would be a great uprising from below. Only if the upper classes were subjected to "the dictatorship of democracy" would it be possible to avert such a catastrophe. If given the necessary power by the Provisional Government, he promised to put through this program in an expeditious manner.

A Rebuff for Verkhovsky.   To these proposals, however, Kerensky and his government turned a deaf ear. Kerensky still sought to provide a government for all men, which would be above all classes. Inevitably this meant opposing the elemental demands of the populace and siding with the upper classes, with whom his sentiments bound him. As for the propertied elements, they were losing their enthusiasm for the war, which instinctively, they realized, Russia could not win. But they refused to draw the inevitable conclusion that Russia should stop fighting.

Konstantin Nabokov, a Cadet, related that in the spring of 1917 Miliukov rejected the idea that weariness with the war was the cause of Russia's ills. "Who knows, perhaps it is thanks to the war that everything still hangs together, and without the war it would have broken down more quickly." Possibly the upper classes, even though they realized that Russia had lost the war, felt that it was essential not to withdraw from the conflict. It may well be that they felt that a cessation of the war would release the pentup forces of revolution and bring the social changes that they feared so desperately. At any rate, whatever the reason, Kerensky's cabinet would not accept Verkhovsky's proposals for a defensive war and for social reforms. In fact, the general himself was now *persona non grata*. Rumors began to circulate that he had suggested a separate peace and that he wished to become dictator. Kerensky failed to support him and he was soon dropped from the government.

The Failure of the Socialist Revolutionaries. Kerensky's failure to take advantage of the collapse of the Right was paralleled by the failure of his party—the Socialist Revolutionaries. This party, the largest political organization in Russia before the revolution, expanded enormously after the fall of the Tsar. It had long enjoyed the support of the teeming peasant millions, and now that many of these millions were in uniform and had rifles in their hands their political activity had greatly increased. They joined the Socialist Revolutionary party in such numbers that the party was not able to digest the huge mass. Several of its most effective leaders had died shortly before the revolution, leaving Victor Chernov, a theorist and writer rather than a practical politician, to deal with the vital problems of the times. Other Socialist Revolutionary leaders, especially those like Kerensky, who had represented the party in the Duma, became more and more conservative and lost touch with the masses.

Even more remarkable was the case of Boris Savinkov, a former member of the party's terrorist organization, who became Minister of War under Kerensky and gave his enthusiastic support to Kornilov. Chernov, on the whole, seems to have remained true to his principles, for as Minister of Agriculture under Kerensky he worked earnestly for agrarian reform. He did not, however, receive the support of his fellow Socialist Revolutionaries, and eventually he was forced out of the government as a dangerous radical.

The Split in the Ranks of the SR's. While the Socialist Revolutionary leaders for the most part were becoming more conservative, the rank and file were becoming more and more radical. In May, 1917, the SR's held their Third All-Russian Congress, at which, in spite of a strong tendency of the Right faction to secede, Chernov's program was adopted, calling for a just and speedy peace and for a positive socialist policy of labor and agrarian legislation. This evidence that the bulk of the party wanted to follow a progressive policy was lost on the leaders, except Chernov, who before long was forced from power.

But as the leaders grew more conservative, the rank and file were steadily drawing closer to the program of the Bolsheviks. Although the masses of soldiers and peasants still thought of themselves as Socialist Revolutionaries, their program of immediate peace and all land to the peasants was very close to that of Lenin. The split between the Rightist leaders of the SR's in Petrograd, who upheld Kerensky and opposed radical measures, and the local SR's, who often stirred up the peasants openly to seize the estates of the landlords, was too wide to bridge. Chernov tried to bridge it by criticizing the program of the dominant group, but they invoked a strong resolution of party discipline and he, fearing to split the party on the eve of the elections to the Constituent Assembly, remained a captive of Kerensky's faction. Thus, as the crisis matured, the Socialist Revolutionaries continued to drift.

The Breakdown of the Army and Navy. To the millions of Russian soldiers, suffering from hunger and cold in the trenches, the Kornilov insurrection added a new and more infuriating grievance. The soldiers had been distrustful of their officers, most of whom had taken no part in the struggle for the overthrow of the Tsar. The men were convinced that the war was an imperialistic struggle for Constantinople and Galicia, and when the July offensive was attempted, it confirmed these beliefs. Now they had seen their highest commanders, who had insistently demanded the death penalty as punishment for desertion and mutiny, rise in rebellion against the revolution. Many of the other officers had sought to aid the Kornilov mutiny and few had taken a stand against it. Moreover, after the rank and file of the army, together with the populace of Petrograd, had suppressed this revolt, it became clear that none of the guilty leaders—to say nothing of the lesser culprits—would pay with his life. The soldiers became convinced that, unless proven otherwise, all officers were enemies of the revolution that had given the enlisted man some hope of a better future. The officers were, therefore, their enemies.

The result of this widespread conviction was that the

soldiers began to express their feelings in drastic fashion. (*See Readings Nos. 21 and 22.*) Fraternization with the enemy became common—in part induced by Bolshevik or German propaganda, but often a spontaneous expression of distaste for the business of killing. Any active measures against the enemy were bitterly opposed: when artillerymen, less infected with the mutinous spirit, opened fire on the enemy lines, thus inviting retaliation against the Russian trenches, the Russian infantry cut the telephone wires to the batteries and even beat the gunners if they persisted in firing. Violence against officers increased after the Kornilov affair. Numerous officers were arrested by their men or were forced to resign. In some cases, privates or corporals were elected to replace them. Riots occasionally occurred, in which officers were beaten or killed. Sometimes enlisted men fired into the quarters of their officers at night or threw hand-grenades into the officers' mess. Even the soldiers' committees and the commissars with the troops were not immune from attack if they tried to uphold the authority of the officers.

The Russian navy was an especially radical part of the armed forces. Kronstadt had become a hotbed of revolt early in the revolution and remained so, in spite of all that Kerensky could do. The naval bases at Helsingfors and Sveaborg were also radical. The crews of all the ships of the Baltic fleet were strongly behind the Bolsheviks and would have played a big role in the Kornilov affair if stubborn fighting had developed. The Black Sea fleet, on the other hand, for some time maintained its discipline under Admiral Kolchak, and in the spring of 1917 it even supported the war. But eventually it, too, succumbed to the revolutionary virus. By the middle of June the sailors began disarming their officers. Kolchak threw his sword into the sea rather than give it up and resigned his command in disgust. By October, 1917, the Black Sea fleet was as radical as the Baltic fleet.

The Rising Peasant Movement. In the early days of the revolution the peasants had not taken the law into their own hands, but had apparently decided to wait for the Constituent Assembly to deal with the land problem. In the meantime, Chernov, Minister of Agriculture, took steps to prepare the basis for a future transfer of the land of the landowners to the peasants. But Chernov was

forced from office with little to show for his efforts, and
the Constituent Assembly was repeatedly postponed. The
peasants, whose conviction remained firm that the land
should go to him who tilled it, grew weary of waiting.
After the failure of Kornilov to set up an iron dictatorship, the peasants felt that the danger of harsh repression
had vanished and they grew more ready to act. As deserters from the army trickled back to the villages, more daring leadership was provided to spur the villages on against
the manors. They needed little urging.

The landowners, sensing the coming hurricane, could
do little. Many of them, realizing that their land would
be lost in any case, resolved to contest any legal confiscation of their holdings, perhaps feeling that a violent peasant seizure would at least leave a basis for future claims
for recovery of the property, if things turned out well.
Others, fearing the worst, hastened to sell their broad
acres, in some cases to foreigners, sold their standing
timber, or divided their property among several members
of their families, hoping in one way or another to salvage
something from their property. All this was not lost on
the villagers, who began to insist that the local authorities
take the properties in trust for the peasants, or that sale
and mortgaging of estates be forbidden. When the local
authorities did take over the estates, more friction between landowners and peasants often resulted. In any case,
events moved swiftly.

The Peasant Whirlwind. In the autumn months of
1917 the climax was reached. (*See Reading No. 23.*)
More and more frequently the peasants marched in a
body to the estates of the landowners, broke into the
manor houses, and pillaged without mercy. If the gentry
submitted without resistance, they were usually permitted
to go in peace. The livestock, implements, furniture, and
other useful articles, as well as the land, were divided up
by the peasants, who then usually burned the manors and
other buildings, to make sure that the owners would not
return. Often much wanton damage was done: the leaves
of fine library books were torn out for cigarette paper,
and paintings by famous artists were cut from their frames
to make canvas trousers.

In the main agricultural provinces of Russia these
scenes were repeated over and over again, until few

nobles had escaped deprivation. In the northern provinces such seizures were rarer, as the nobility were fewer and their lands less valuable. In October, the attacks on the estates of the nobility reached epidemic proportions, amounting in one month alone almost to the total for the preceding seven months. Sometimes the landowners appealed for military protection, and in places troops were sent to their aid. During the summer of 1917, these measures proved effective, but in the autumn months the sending of troops availed little. The soldiers, almost ninety per cent of them peasants, strongly sympathized with their brethren and often refused to act against them. There even were occasions where the soldiers actually aided the peasants in driving out the landowners, and in a few cases they joined them in hunting down the owner with their bayonets.

Even in October, 1917, the peasants still thought of themselves as followers of the Socialist Revolutionaries and did not realize that the program they were carrying out was advocated by Lenin. Nevertheless, the Bolsheviks had no reason to fear that the peasants would oppose their seizure of power or would rally to the support of the Provisional Government.

The Upsurge of the Workers. The factory workers had been, from the beginning of the revolution, the most radical element in Russia. Repeatedly, in Petrograd, the proletarians had given proof of their readiness to seek an extreme solution of their difficulties. After the frustration of the masses in the July Days, the workers had been somewhat subdued, and their units of Red Guards had been largely disarmed by the government. But their grievances had not been remedied, but rather had become more burdensome as the galloping inflation cut sharply into the buying power of their wages. Food riots grew increasingly frequent. (*See Readings No. 24 and 25.*)

To make matters worse, after midsummer there were increasingly frequent closings of factories, which threw harassed men out of work. Probably, in most cases, these shutdowns were caused by such unavoidable factors as shortages of fuel or raw materials like steel, rubber, and cotton. But the desperate workers were always prone to think that the closings were lockouts intended to compel the workers to reduce their wage demands, especially as the employers were known to have expressed wrath on this score. The remark allegedly made by Riabushinsky, a great industrialist, rang from one end of Russia to the other: "Perhaps . . . we need the bony hand of hunger, the poverty of the people, which would seize by the throat all these false friends of the people, all those democratic Soviets and committees." Whether it was said or not, it was widely believed, and it infuriated the workers, who needed little to anger them.

As their passions rose, many of the workers turned to violence against their employers—in Petrograd, in Moscow, in the Donets Basin of the eastern Ukraine, and in other places. Numerous instances were reported in the press. Shots were fired at factory administrators, they were arrested for refusing to raise wages, executives were ousted or barricaded in their offices. In one factory in the south, workers beat a managing engineer and carted him out in a wheelbarrow. The government could do little to stem the tide. Furthermore, in a number of cases where factories shut down, the workers seized the plants and tried to run them, making strenuous efforts to obtain fuel, raw materials, or orders for the products, and in that way to earn their bread. While these efforts may not have been very effective, they clearly showed that the industrial workers were in a revolutionary frame of mind.

The Rising Power of the Bolsheviks.   With soldiers, peasants, and workers in a militant frame of mind, the Bolsheviks found themselves in a steadily improving position. They could gain little support among the peasants, but the soldiers, both at the front and in the garrisons in the rear, were turning to them and rejecting less radical advisers. Likewise the workers, who had never believed the charges against Lenin, in the fall of 1917 almost completely gave their allegiance to the Bolsheviks. Lenin had urged his party to concentrate on getting control of the factory committees, which proved to be relatively easy. The committees, which gave strong support to the demands of the workers, won many of them from the influence of the trade unions, which were largely controlled by the Mensheviks. But the trade unions themselves were not proof against the rising Bolshevik sentiment, and in the fall months they, too, began to come under Bolshevik control. The railway workers and the printers remained loyal to the Mensheviks, but by November many of the other unions were already Bolshevik.

Control of the workers and the garrison troops led inevitably to control of the Soviets through their frequent elections. On September 12 the Bolsheviks obtained a majority in the Petrograd Soviet, and on October 8 it elected Trotsky as its president. The Moscow Soviet was won by the Bolsheviks on September 18, and many of the provincial Soviets were coming under their control.

The party of Lenin was strong not only in the two capitals, but also in the Volga towns, the industrial centers of the Urals, the Donets Basin, and in other industrial towns of the Ukraine. Moreover, the Bolsheviks had as allies the Left Socialist Revolutionaries, who had a considerable following in the army and among the peasants. Thus, the Bolsheviks had effective support in many important areas of Russia and need no longer fear that a Red Petrograd would be opposed by the rest of the country.

Lenin's Insistence on an Uprising.   Lenin, still in Finland, was immensely cheered by the results of the Kornilov insurrection. In the latter part of September, he wrote a letter to the Central Committee of the Bolshevik party demanding the seizure of power and reviving the slogan "All Power to the Soviets." This letter, however, was promptly rejected by the Central Committee as unrealistic. He followed this with two secret letters to the Central Committee saying that the time was ripe for seizure. His arguments, however, failed to sway the committee. Moreover, his objections to participation in the Democratic Conference, although backed by Trotsky and Stalin, were opposed by Kamenev and Rykov, who swung the Central Committee to approve taking part.

This setback failed to discourage Lenin, however. Early in October he moved to the Finnish city of Vyborg to be nearer Petrograd, the scene of action. Another letter, "The Crisis Is Ripe," repeated his earlier arguments that the Bolsheviks now had strong support from the masses and added a new argument: the revolution in Germany, he declared, was fast approaching and would back up the revolt in Russia. To show his sincerity and determination, Lenin offered his resignation to the Central Committee in order that he might have freedom of action. The offer was refused, but Lenin continued to oppose the decision of his party by writing to various local organizations of the Bolsheviks and to the populace to urge support for his program. (*See Reading No. 26.*)

One of Lenin's most effective strokes was a pamphlet, *Can the Bolsheviks Hold State Power?* In it he strove to refute the arguments of some of the more moderate Bolsheviks, who held that, even if an insurrection should prove successful, it would not be supported by the rest of the country and in the end would be drowned in a sea of blood. Lenin, however, argued that if a few hundred thousand landowners and Tsarist officials could rule Russia for centuries, the Bolsheviks, who already enjoyed the support of great masses of the people, could hold power. Especially, he stated, when the lowly and the poor began to see that the new Soviet government would suppress the rich and strip them of their wealth, which would be given to the needy poor, then "no power of the capitalists and kulaks . . . can conquer the people's revolution."

Gradually, Lenin's persistent urging won out over the doubts of his fellow Bolsheviks. On October 22, he returned to Petrograd in disguise and on the following day he spoke at a crucial meeting of the Central Committee. His passionate emphasis on the need for an uprising and his reproaches of "indifference" to this question turned the tide in his favor, albeit with difficulty. The vote was ten to two in favor of an insurrection, with Zinoviev and Kamenev opposed. The Central Committee also named a Political Bureau to carry out the preparations for the revolt.

Stalin's Role in 1917. In the 1930's Stalin claimed that during 1917 he had been Lenin's righthand man. This was far from accurate, as was the contrary allegation by Trotsky and others that he was a nonentity. Stalin had had a long and fairly successful career as an aggressive labor leader and organizer in the Caucasus, thanks to which he had come to Lenin's notice. As a result, Lenin had Stalin named as member of the Bolshevik Central Committee in 1912. Shortly thereafter, he was made one of the four-man Russian Bureau, which directed party affairs in Russia, and for a short time edited the party newspaper *Pravda.* In 1913 he visited Lenin briefly in Cracow, Austria, and at his suggestion wrote an article on the minority problem. On his return to Russia, however, he was arrested and exiled to northern Siberia, where he remained until early 1917. After his return to Petrograd he quickly gave his allegiance to Lenin. Although not a well known figure, he again edited *Pravda* and served on the Central Committee. For a time, in midsummer, 1917, when Lenin and other leaders were in hiding or in prison, Stalin was a key man, but Trotsky and other chieftains soon superseded him. On the eve of the insurrection Stalin became a member of the new seven-man Political Bureau. Nevertheless, except for his editorial duties and his participation in deciding party strategy, his actual part in the Bolshevik Revolution was small.

Continued Opposition to Lenin's Policy. Lenin's victory on October 23 did not by any means silence the opposition or win invariable success for his proposals. Much to his disgust, the Bolshevik members of the Democratic Conference resolved by a vote of 72 to 50 to participate in the next *ad hoc* gathering, the Council of the Republic. This body, formed in part from the Democratic Conference, and in part from other organizations, contained representatives of all parties, both Right and Left. It was to function as an advisory body to the Provisional Government and also to prepare the agenda for the Constituent Assembly, which had finally been set for December. By the time of the first meeting of the Council of the Republic (also known as the Pre-Parliament) on October 20, the Bolsheviks had decided to walk out of the assembly on the opening day. The exit occurred after a bitter denunciation of the Provisional Government by Trotsky, charging that the government, by prolonging the war, was causing the needless slaughter of hundreds of thousands. He closed with a ringing declaration that the Bolsheviks had nothing in common "with this government of treason to the people and this Council of complicity in counter-revolution," and gave a call for all power to the Soviets.

On October 29, Lenin again presented his arguments to an enlarged meeting of the Central Committee. He told the Bolsheviks that there would be either a dictatorship of the Right or the Left, and that the party should not be guided solely by the feelings of the masses, who were inclined to waver from one side to the other. He also expressed faith in the coming German revolution. Once more he won, but again Zinoviev and Kamenev voiced their doubts, which may have been shared by others present. Kamenev then resigned from the Central Committee. Two days later a letter from Zinoviev and Kamenev appeared in Maxim Gorky's *Novaia Zhizn*, announcing that the Bolsheviks were preparing an armed uprising, which the signers felt was a dangerous mistake. Lenin, infuriated, condemned their action as "strike-breaking" and "a crime." He followed this up with a letter to the Central Committee, which met without him on November 2, asking that the two be expelled from the party.

Nevertheless, an effort was made to patch the matter up. Kamenev resigned from the Central Committee, which enjoined the two members to refrain from further public opposition to the policy of the party. Lenin's demand for their expulsion from the party was not dealt with. Lenin seems to have been satisfied with the action taken, for on November 6, when the Central Committee met to prepare for the revolutionary action on the morrow, Kamenev resumed his seat as though he had never resigned. Lenin's policy was about to be applied.

— 8 —

THE OVERTHROW OF THE PROVISIONAL GOVERNMENT

Bolshevik Preparations. The Bolshevik leaders, who, on October 23, had decided to undertake an armed insurrection, at first did little to prepare for it. On October 22, a proposal of the Mensheviks for the formation of a Military Revolutionary Committee to coordinate the defense of Petrograd, chiefly against the advancing Germans, offered a convenient way to organize the uprising.

The Military Revolutionary Committee, as it was finally set up by the Petrograd Soviet, became a sort of general staff for the insurrection. Thanks to a boycott of the committee by the moderate socialists, the Bolsheviks completely controlled it. The Left Socialist Revolutionaries and Anarchists in the committee deferred to the Bolsheviks. Thus, the latter, headed by Trotsky, were able freely to prepare the troops of the garrison of Petrograd and of the surrounding towns, to expand and equip the Red Guards, and in other ways to get ready.

When an effort was made, late in October, to send some of the Petrograd garrison to the front, the Military Revolutionary Committee won the fervent gratitude of the soldiers by opposing the transfer. The Committee sent revolutionary commissars to all the regiments of the garrison, driving out the government's commissars, and thus obtaining control of all the armed forces. Inevitably, the Military Revolutionary Committee clashed with the staff of the Petrograd Military District and appealed to the soldiers for their support against the staff. (*See Reading No. 27.*)

In addition, the Bolsheviks unceasingly sent out their best speakers to the barracks and the factories to whip up the enthusiasm of the masses for the insurrection. Trotsky proved especially effective in inspiring the people. On November 4, the Day of the Petrograd Soviet, when there was a great outpouring of workers and soldiers and other members of the lower orders to meetings organized all over Petrograd, Trotsky succeeded in arousing his audience to transports of enthusiasm for the coming events. (*See Reading No. 28.*)

The Fortress of Peter and Paul, which sprawled on the river bank across from the Winter Palace, appeared to be an obstacle to Bolshevik success. After many discussions as to how to win control of its neutral garrison, Trotsky, on November 5, casually went to the fortress and, finding a soldiers' meeting in progress, promptly addressed it. The soldiers, who were probably wavering already, needed little urging to join the insurrectionary forces. Thus, one of the government's main strongholds fell without a shot being fired. Moreover, the arsenal of Peter and Paul contained large stocks of rifles, which were promptly turned over to the Red Guards, who were among the most active forces at the disposal of the Military Revolutionary Committee.

Thus, the preparations of the Bolsheviks were energetically pushed in the days before the Second Congress of Soviets. This gathering had originally been planned for October. But the Central Executive Committee, composed of moderate socialists, realized that the Congress would probably have a Bolshevik majority and, hence, they hesitated to call it. The Bolsheviks, however, were so insistent that it meet that finally it was set for November 2. It was again postponed to the 7th by the reluctant government, and it was this date that was chosen for the seizure of power.

The Government's Course of Action. While the headquarters of the Military Revolutionary Committee seethed with active preparations for an armed uprising, the Provisional Government did very little. Certainly the coming uprising was no secret, as few were in ignorance of the plans of the Bolsheviks. As early as October 7 *Riech,* the leading Cadet newspaper, spoke of the danger of "a cannibal triumph of the Lenins." In the Petrograd and Moscow Soviets, Bolshevik members were compelled to give evasive answers to the frequent questions as to whether they were planning to come out in rebellion. As the final day drew nearer and nearer, the non-Bolshevik press assumed an air of confidence. On November 3 *Riech* announced: "If the Bolsheviks venture to come out they will be crushed without difficulty." A Menshevik paper declared that the garrison and proletariat of Petrograd were isolated from the rest of the people, while Maxim Gorky's leftist journal declared that only the followers of Kornilov would benefit from a revolt.

Kerensky, whose health was impaired, seems to have done little to forestall an uprising. Late in October, he went off to Headquarters for several days. At this time, one of his ministers investigated the government's measures against a possible insurrection, only to find that no significant steps had been taken. Yet, early in November, Kerensky, when asked by a leading Cadet about the government's readiness to meet a crisis, replied: "I could pray that such an uprising would take place. I have more strength than I need. They will finally be crushed." Actually, Colonel Polkovnikov, commander at Petrograd, had been very careful to avoid a clash with the Military Revolutionary Committee, even when it defied his authority over the troops. Perhaps the fact that the Petrograd Soviet had been interfering with the garrison ever since the fall of the Tsar, and the failure of the July Days and other Bolshevik demonstrations, had convinced the Colonel that Bolshevik influence over troops and populace was merely a familiar aspect of the revolutionary scene, which was of little importance.

The Government Acts. Finally, in a meeting on November 5, the government decided to strike against the Bolshevik menace. The forces of junkers (military cadets) in Petrograd were to be called out to close the Bolshevik newspapers, to arrest the leading Bolsheviks, and to subdue the Military Revolutionary Committee. Reliable troops were to be brought to the capital, including junkers from the school at Oranienbaum, shock troops, and artillery. On November 6, the government forces moved. The junkers seized the printing shop where *Pravda* was published, scattered the type, and confiscated some 8,000 copies. The cruiser *Aurora,* anchored in the Neva near the Winter Palace, was ordered to put to sea for a training cruise. A Woman's Battalion of Death moved into the Winter Palace, the seat of the government, along with some junkers and a few Cossacks. Junkers seized and raised several of the main bridges and occupied important government buildings, including the main telephone and postal building. This show of force, like many of the actions of the Provisional Government, was both ineffectual and late. The reaction was immediate and strong.

The Attack on the Provisional Government. The Military Revolutionary Committee at once counter-attacked. Troops were ordered to retake and guard the printing establishments, which by 11 o'clock were again in Red hands. The orders to the *Aurora* were countermanded, and it again dropped anchor. Sailors from its crew landed and helped the Red Guards seize and lower the bridges.

Little more happened on that day, however, as both sides mustered their forces for the final test. Kerensky turned to the Council of the Republic for support. To his disappointment, however, it approved a proposal by Mar-

tov, a Menshevik leader, which, while it condemned the
uprising, demanded that the government give the lands
of the nobility to the peasants and insisted on immediate
steps toward peace. Kerensky, however, refused to accept
what was a carbon copy of Lenin's program, and he left
the Council vowing to smash the revolt.

The Bolsheviks also met on November 6 to plan their
strategy. It was decided to assign troops to guard the
junker garrisons of the public buildings, while the workers
were being assembled for offensive action. Finally, the
Winter Palace was to be attacked by sailors from Kronstadt and by the Red Guards. Orders were also issued
for the uprising to start in Moscow.

At night the Red forces moved to attack, quickly over-
running the main railway stations and the remaining
bridges. Torpedo boats from the Baltic fleet moved into
the Neva to aid in the assault. On the morning of November 7, the State Bank and the main telephone station were
taken, with very little bloodshed. The government now
held little of the city but the Winter Palace. The vastly
superior forces of the attackers and their high discipline
had overwhelmed the weak and dispirited defenders. It
must be said, however, that the Red forces were poorly
led, as for hours they failed to make use of their opportunity to crush the defenders at once. But not even the
gift of much precious time could save the government.

Kerensky's Flight.   In the interim Kerensky was in
the Winter Palace trying to obtain reinforcements. Several
regiments of Don Cossacks promised their support, but
failed to appear. When Kerensky telephoned them over a
secret wire that was still functioning, they repeatedly
assured him that they "were getting ready to saddle the
horses." But the horses were never saddled. Likewise,
Kerensky's own party, the Socialist Revolutionaries, could
provide him with no armed forces.

Eventually, therefore, the Premier realized that the
government's position was hopeless and decided to flee
Petrograd, hoping to bring back troops to retake the
capital. One of his aides requisitioned a car belonging to
a Secretary of the American Embassy, and thus, flying
the American flag, Kerensky escaped through the Bolshevik patrols to go for help.

The Fall of the Winter Palace.   The Bolsheviks

moved slowly to the kill. They gradually occupied the whole city, which scarcely realized what was happening. Street cars and theaters were functioning as in normal times. Early in the afternoon of the 7th the Council of the Republic was surrounded by troops, which ordered it to leave the building. The delegates had no choice but to submit after registering a formal protest for the record.

The insurgents moved slowly toward the Winter Palace and, early in the evening, summoned it to surrender. Most of the military men there, realizing the hopelessness of the situation, urged acceptance, but the ministers refused to submit. They shut themselves up in the palace, defended by a small force of junkers and the Woman's Battalion of Death. Barricades of firewood were thrown up in the palace square, and the tiny force settled down for a siege. Part of the garrison had already slipped away, and the morale of those that remained was not high.

The attack was long delayed. The threat to use the guns of the ships and the artillery of the Fortress proved empty, as the Fortress gunners had no wish to fire. Only a few shells were fired by the *Aurora*, most of them doing little damage. The assault of the troops was relatively bloodless, as neither side was out for blood. (*See Reading No. 29.*)

For the most part the fighting consisted of rather aimless firing, while groups of men filtered in through the innumerable entrances to the palace. At first, the defenders were able to disarm the attackers, but as the latter increased in numbers they succeeded in disarming the garrison.

Finally, the last remnants of junkers sought to stand outside the inner room where the ministers were sitting, but they were quickly ordered to surrender. Antonov, the Red leader, promptly arrested the ministers and sent them off under guard to the Fortress of Peter and Paul. Passing through the infuriated crowd, they were almost lynched, but their guards succeeded in delivering them unharmed. A few days later they were put under house arrest in their homes, and before long they were given their freedom. The revolution was still relatively humane.

There was still opposition to the Bolshevik revolution in Petrograd. The moderate socialists—Mensheviks and

Socialist Revolutionaries—resigned from the Congress of Soviets in protest against the overthrow of the government. After vainly trying a protest march, they withdrew to the city Duma, where, with delegates from the Council of the Republic and the old Central Executive Committee, they formed a Committee for the Salvation of the Fatherland and the Revolution. But it could do little but issue angry protests and appeal for support against the lawless action of the Bolsheviks. The new revolutionary regime held Petrograd.

Kerensky's Attempt to Retake the Capital.   Kerensky, having made his escape on November 7, arrived at Pskov, headquarters of the Northern Front, that night. Here he joined General P. N. Krasnov, who was willing to march on Petrograd. By November 12 they had occupied Tsarskoe Selo, a day's march from the capital. But they had only some 700 Cossacks, a few guns, and an armored car. An uprising of junkers in Petrograd occurred on the 11th, but was easily put down, and when Krasnov pushed against the city's defenses the next day, his tiny force was repulsed by sailors and Red Guards. Threatened in the flank and rear by other large forces, he had to retreat. Eventually, his men, shaken by Soviet propaganda, signed an armistice. Kerensky was almost captured, but thanks to a friendly Socialist Revolutionary he was able to escape in disguise and finally made his way to England. General Krasnov was arrested by Red troops on November 15 and taken to Petrograd. He was soon released on parole, and before long made his way to the Don, where he later became leader of the Don Cossack anti-Bolshevik movement. Thus, for the present, the revolutionary regime in Petrograd was secure against attack.

The Revolution in the Rest of Russia.   In Moscow, in contrast to Petrograd, there was long and stubborn fighting. The Moscow Bolsheviks, led by less determined men than Lenin and Trotsky, were slow in preparing for revolt, and it was only on November 7 that a Military Revolutionary Committee was set up. The anti-Bolshevik forces rallied around a Committee of Public Safety behind junkers who held the main part of the city. A Soviet force in the Kremlin was isolated by the junkers, who were in turn blockaded by the much larger forces of soldiers and Red Guards in the outlying parts of the city.

On November 9 and 10, the junkers occupied many of the strategic points in the city and persuaded the commandant of the Kremlin to surrender. But the Red forces gradually closed in on the Whites, and as reenforcements kept coming for the Reds the junkers lost heart. By the 14th the Red forces had taken many key positions, and only the Kremlin held out. After an artillery bombardment it was stormed by Red Guards on November 15, and the remaining resistance was soon overcome. Moscow was securely in Red hands.

In the rest of the country, especially in the main Russian areas, the change in power occurred more easily. Although in some places it took weeks, it was almost bloodless, as there were few to fight for the fallen government. In some of the minority areas, however, more enduring opposition regimes were set up. In Transcaucasia the Bolsheviks, aided by the oil-workers of Baku, easily set up Soviet rule in Azerbaidzhan, but in Tiflis the Georgian Mensheviks maintained a moderate, highly nationalist government. In several of the Cossack regions, especially the Urals, the Don, and the Kuban, military regimes were established which opposed the Soviet government.

The Ukraine proved to be an especially troublesome area. In the eastern and southern parts the population, partly Russian and largely proletarian, set up a Ukrainian Soviet in Kharkov, but in Kiev Soviet authority failed to gain control. At first, the Soviet forces with much difficulty drove out a force of junkers and officers, only to have the Ukrainian *Rada* step in and occupy the city. With the Ukrainian troops under its control, the *Rada* disarmed the Red Guards and proclaimed the Ukraine a People's Republic, with the *Rada* the sole authority for the whole Ukraine. This claim was rejected by the Soviet in Kharkov, which declared that *it* represented the whole Ukraine. But, for the time being, the *Rada* held Kiev and the western part against the Soviet government in Petrograd.

The Struggle for Army Headquarters. While the fighting in Petrograd was going on, Kerensky asked General N. N. Dukhonin, the commander-in-chief, to send troops to the aid of the government. He did what he could, but many of the troops refused to go, and others were stranded by the railway men and won over by Bolshevik propaganda. The various army commanders also found they could not fight the Soviet government, and threw in their lot with it. As a result, after demanding a cessation of fighting and unconditional submission to the Provisional Government, Dukhonin, on November 14, changed his tune and halted all troop movements toward Petrograd. For a time, there was a truce between Dukhonin and the Soviet authorities.

On November 20, 1917, the Red government ordered Dukhonin to ask the German high command for an armistice. (*See Reading No. 30.*) Hearing nothing from him, on November 22 Lenin and Ensign N. N. Krylenko, the new commander-in-chief, called him on the direct wire to ask what progress he had made. At first evasive, Dukhonin later answered that he could not comply, as only a legally established government could make peace. Thereupon, Lenin dismissed him, ordering him, however, to carry on routine work until Krylenko could arrive to take over.

The next day Krylenko, accompanied by a convoy of sailors, set out for Headquarters, stopping en route to remove uncooperative generals. Dukhonin, an old-style officer with little imagination, now found himself deluged with advice from all sides. The revolutionary leaders and troops insisted that he submit to the Soviet regime. On the other hand, the chiefs of the Allied Military Missions at Headquarters sent him a strong note warning him not to make an armistice or a separate peace and threatening him with "most serious consequences" if Russia violated her treaties with her allies. While this was an empty gesture, Dukhonin seems to have been impressed, for he stayed where he was. Although the news grew alarming as Krylenko advanced in triumph toward Headquarters, Dukhonin apparently felt that his picked troops would bar the way to the Red commander.

In the meantime, Chernov and several other prominent Socialist Revolutionary leaders had reached Headquarters, where the General Army Committee proposed a new government, headed by Chernov. He accepted the dubious honor. Later, however, he and his colleagues realized the hopelessness of the situation and quietly returned to Petrograd to await the Constituent Assembly. Dukhonin foolishly lingered on.

On December 1, the local Soviet took power in the head-quarters city and named a Military Revolutionary Committee. The shock troops left the same day. When Krylenko arrived on December 3, the unfortunate Dukhonin was brought as a prisoner to his car. A mob of soldiers, sailors, and peasants gathered, demanding that the prisoner be dispatched on the spot. Krylenko spoke out strongly against a lynching and succeeded in calming the crowd. He soon went on, however, and after he had gone the crowd, again aroused by vengeful orators, dragged Dukhonin out on the platform and beat him to death.

Thus, the attempt to use the army as a center of opposition failed. The Soviet government proceeded to establish complete control over all the command posts, so that a threat from that direction was no longer possible. Indeed, the army as an organized force was rapidly going out of existence, as a vast flood of deserters moved homeward. Only the Cossacks, the Georgians, and the *Rada* remained in defiance of the Soviet authorities. They, indeed, were too weak to be a threat, as they were menaced by attack from the sketchy Soviet military forces. The Soviet government was accepted throughout the rest of the vast territory of Russia, and no effective challenge to its power was visible anywhere in this expanse.

— 9 —

THE FIRST MEASURES OF THE SOVIET GOVERNMENT

First Steps of the New Regime. On November 7, while the fighting for Petrograd was still going on, Lenin made his first public appearance before the Petrograd Soviet. (*See Reading No. 31.*) To it he proclaimed in triumph the coming of "the workers' and peasants' revolution" which he had long predicted. He then sketched the immediate program of the victors: the destruction of the old governing machine and the creation of a new one, the immediate ending of the war, and the satisfying of the peasants by a decree wiping out the property rights of the nobility. Then, turning to the international scene, he hailed the movement of the workers "which is already beginning to develop in Italy, England, and Germany," and closed with the cry: "Long live the world socialist revolution!"

Secession of the Moderates. Lenin did not appear before the Second Congress of Soviets when it met that evening. As had been expected, it was predominantly Bolshevik: some 390 out of the total membership of 850 were followers of Lenin, with more than 100 of the Left Socialist Revolutionaries, who were allied with the Bolsheviks. There were not more than 80 Mensheviks, including members of the Jewish *Bund,* while the pro-Kerensky Socialist Revolutionaries had a mere 60 delegates. From the beginning, the moderates refused to accept the revolutionary overturn and bitterly denounced the insurrection as treason to the revolution. (*See Reading No. 32.*) Representatives of the army joined the attack by terming the uprising a betrayal of the army and a crime against the people. The Mensheviks, the Socialist Revolutionaries, and the Bund followed these utterances by walking out of the Congress in protest against the revolt, whose cannon could be heard in the distance. The protestors went to the city Duma and joined the Committee for Salvation of the Fatherland and the Revolution. Many of the remaining members of the Congress were dismayed at the secession of the moderates, but Trotsky hastened to express the feelings of many that the revolt was an insurrection, not a conspiracy, and that it expressed the will of the masses of Russia. To the backs of the retreating delegates he flung the contemptuous phrase that they were "refuse that will be swept into the garbage can of history."

The Congress continued its session until early morning. Before it adjourned it heard of the fall of the Winter Palace and received reports that important bodies of troops had promised their support. Its chief work at this session was a proclamation to the people sketching the program of the new regime and asking their earnest support. (*See Reading No. 33.*)

Lenin's Proposals. Lenin, who had spent the night resting beside Trotsky, appeared before the Congress of Soviets on November 8. After several preliminary speeches, Lenin rose, to receive a loud ovation. He then read a "proclamation to the peoples and the governments of all the fighting nations." (*See Reading No. 34.*) It contained a pledge to abolish secret diplomacy and to publish immediately the secret treaties with the Allies, as well as a renunciation of the special privileges granted to Russia. The proclamation went on to propose an armistice lasting three months, and appealed to the working people of England, France, and Germany to take "decisive, energetic, and persistent action" to bring about a successful peace and at the same time to achieve the liberation of the masses of exploited working people "from all slavery and exploitation." After a brief discussion the proposal was adopted with vast enthusiasm: one delegate who ventured to vote against it felt it safer to drop his opposition. The Congress then sang the *"Internationale,"* the anthem of international revolutionary socialism.

The next point on the agenda was land for the peasants. A short decree proposed by Lenin (*see Reading No. 35*) abolished private landholding at once and without compensation. Private, state, crown, and church lands were to be turned over to land committees and Soviets of Peasants' Deputies for distribution to the peasants. The rules for the distribution of the land were set forth in an Instruction appended to the decree. The Instruction, which Lenin had obtained from a compilation of peasant resolutions prepared by the Soviet of Peasants' Deputies, provided for a complete ban on private ownership of land, prohibition of the buying and selling of land, and for the use of the land solely by persons who would work it with their own and their families' labor. This measure, which would promote a mass of small peasant farms, was contrary to accepted Marxist views. Hence, there was some objection to it from Bolshevik members of the Congress. Lenin, however, frankly stated that this was a Socialist Revolutionary proposal which he felt it necessary to adopt in order to win the support of the peasant masses. On this basis, the Congress approved it.

The Formation of the Soviet Government. While the above measures were readily approved, it proved more difficult to form the revolutionary government. In spite of the secession of the moderate socialists and their opposition to the revolutionary overturn, the Left Socialist Revolutionaries and the Menshevik Internationalists were extremely eager to have a coalition of all socialist parties instead of a purely Leftist government. Likewise *Vikzhel*, the railway workers' union, insisted on a coalition, threatening to stop all rail traffic unless agreement were reached. The demand for an all-socialist government was also warmly endorsed by many of the Bolsheviks. Consequently, in spite of the scorn of Lenin and Trotsky for the moderates, it was necessary to try to form a coalition. But while this was being attempted a government was needed, and so an all-Bolshevik cabinet was set up. Several posts were offered to the Left Socialist Revolutionaries, but they refused to enter the government. So the Council of People's Commissars was approved, with Lenin as President, Trotsky as Commissar for Foreign Affairs, and Rykov as Commissar for Internal Affairs. Most of the other appointees were men who were not well known; among them was Joseph Stalin, Commissar for Nationalities.

A Coalition Government? The possibilities of a coalition regime were explored at length at a conference that met on November 11, 1917. The negotiations lasted for some time, but because of the stiff demands of the moderate socialists they produced no result. At first the socialists insisted that the Military Revolutionary Committee be dissolved and that Lenin and Trotsky be excluded from the government. Later, after the Bolsheviks had consolidated their power in both Moscow and Petrograd, there was less pressure for a coalition and Lenin was able to overcome the moderate Bolsheviks. Nevertheless, on November 17, five of the Bolsheviks of the Central Committee—among them Zinoviev, Kamenev, and Rykov—resigned in protest against the rejection of a coalition. There were also resignations from the cabinet over the same issue.

Lenin was not dismayed by this revolt within his party. He answered it with a furious manifesto from the Central Committee upholding his course and terming the dissenters "waverers and doubters." Such men counted for little, he said, when the Soviet government was supported by "millions of workers in the towns, soldiers in the trenches, peasants in the villages, ready to achieve at any cost the victory of peace and the victory of socialism." This ended the revolt.

None the less, in November the Bolsheviks reached an understanding with the Left Socialist Revolutionaries, and 108 delegates from the Peasant Congress were added to the Soviet Executive Committee. On December 22, the Left Socialist Revolutionaries accepted three posts in the Council of People's Commissars. Thus, a coalition of a sort was finally established, although not so broad in its makeup as the one that had been demanded.

Miscellaneous Actions of the Soviet Government. From the first days of its existence, the new government wrestled with a whole series of problems and wrote a remarkable record of achievements—many of which, it must be said, existed only on paper. Almost immediately there was a sweeping strike of government workers, who refused to recognize the new order. For a regime without a shred of experience in governing this proved most difficult, especially as the State Bank was among the striking institutions. For days the government could obtain no funds, and only the use of force and the opening of the vaults made money available to the Bolshevik rulers of Russia. On December 27, all banks were nationalized and occupied by forces of troops, while the vaults and safe deposit boxes were opened by a commissar. Eventually, the funds of the striking civil servants ran out and they returned to duty in January, 1918.

Economic Measures. During the first few months, decrees flowed forth in a rapid stream. One of the first was a decree directed to the working people, informing them that economic power had been transferred to them. (*See Reading No. 36.*) The nationalization of banks was next, followed by a ban on dividends and securities. On February 10, 1918, a decree annulled all debts of the Russian government, including foreign debts. Contrary to Bolshevik doctrine, Lenin was in no hurry to nationalize industry and even wanted the managerial personnel to continue to work on fairly generous terms. Nevertheless, "workers' control" meant supervision and much outright interference by the workers, so that the conditions in the factories became chaotic. When this led to the shutting down of enterprises, the Supreme Economic Council, created on December 15, had the power to nationalize them.

There was a general levelling down of the standard of living—in part by the ever rising inflation, and in part by decree: members of the Council of Commissars were restricted to 500 rubles per month, with allowances for dependants, and to one room for each member of the family. The ending of private ownership of multiple dwellings was another levelling measure: the city Soviets took them over and sought to equalize the housing facilities, often moving families from the slums into the half-empty apartments of wealthy citizens. The food situation proved to be the most insoluble problem. Try as they would, the Soviet authorities could not obtain more bread for the cities, and the amounts issued on rations fell drastically. To the hungry workers there was left only the consolation that the hated "bourgeois" were faring even worse than they.

Political and Social Legislation.   Important political and social decrees were also issued during the first months. To cope with secret enemies of the regime, drunken mobs that invaded mansions in search of liquor, and food speculators, on December 20 Felix Dzerzhinsky, a fanatical Polish Communist, became head of the All-Russian Extraordinary Commission, whose name, abbreviated to *Cheka,* became dreaded throughout Russia. A system of revolutionary tribunals was set up to deal with political cases, while new, informal "people's courts" dispensed ordinary justice by common sense rather than law books. The Soviet legislators also found time to reform the Russian alphabet and the calendar. Sweeping new laws made marriage and divorce equally easy to obtain and legalized all children, whether born of registered or informal unions. The full legal equality of men and women was also proclaimed.

The Church and the Revolution.   The Russian Orthodox church, which had had a privileged status under the old regime, was extremely hostile to the Bolshevik revolution. While the overthrow of the Kerensky regime was still in progress, a Council or *Sobor* of the church in Moscow was electing a Patriarch as its head. Although the other religious denominations did not oppose the revolution, the Sobor at once issued a message to the people calling on them to repent and to turn from the false counselors who had led them astray. The Soviet government did not, however, react to this.

Nevertheless, many of the measures of the new regime angered the churchmen, who hoped ardently for its overthrow, and on February 1, 1918, the Patriarch issued a pastoral letter to the people. It strongly indicted the Soviet leaders for having caused violence and outrages. "Your acts are not merely cruel, they are the works of Satan, for which you will burn in hell fire in the life hereafter. . . ." To this he added his anathema. To the believers, he issued a call to organize in defense of the church, for "the gates of Hell shall not prevail against it." (*See Reading No. 37.*)

This, however, did not deter the Soviet authorities, who on February 5, 1918, published a law by which "the church was separated from the state, and the school from the church." (*See Reading No. 38.*) Religion was made a private matter for the citizens, and no religious functions or ceremonies were permitted in any institution of government, whether national or local. Religious teaching was barred from all schools, public and private alike. Even the theological schools were ordered closed. The property of churches and religious societies was nationalized, although church buildings might be turned over to congregations of believers for free use for public worship.

This measure was strongly opposed by the leaders of the Orthodox church, but, in spite of their angry protests, the government put it into effect. There were some demonstrations in opposition to it, and occasional riots, at times accompanied by bloodshed. But the government persisted in its purpose. Perhaps the fact that the churches remained open and no attempt was made to prevent divine worship explains why this legislation, which was unfavorable to the Russian church, did not produce any effective explosions of popular wrath.

The Problem of the Constituent Assembly.   One of the worst dilemmas for the Bolsheviks was caused by the Constituent Assembly. The Provisional Government had promised to convene this body speedily, but nothing was done about it for months. Finally, the government set November 25 as the date for the elections. Thus, when the Bolsheviks took power they were in a quandary. Before they had seized power, one of their effective slogans had been for "Speedy Convocation of the Constituent Assembly!" But, while they were on record as wanting it to meet soon, Lenin and the other Bolsheviks had reason to believe that vast numbers of peasants as usual would vote for the Socialist Revolutionaries. It seemed likely that the new Soviet government would be challenged by a body in which the Bolsheviks would be only a minority. Lenin firmly held that the Soviets, which excluded the propertied classes, were a higher form of democracy than a body elected by universal suffrage. His solution was to postpone the elections, but it was decided to hold them and to convene the Assembly, which should, however, be dissolved if it proved troublesome.

The Result of the Elections.   Although the Bolsheviks made no effort to dominate the elections, which began on November 25, the Cadet party was especially handicapped by the fact that many of their leaders were in hiding or in prison, and their newspapers were largely suppressed. The voting gave the Bolsheviks only 175 of the 707 elected members of the Constituent Assembly. The SR's (Socialist Revolutionaries) had 410—a substantial majority—and most of the other delegates were anti-Bolshevik. Yet the figures do not tell the whole story. The Bolsheviks were now in alliance with the Left SR's, who had had a majority of the Peasant Congress. Although the Left SR's had only 40 out of the 410 SR delegates, it seems probable that their following in the country was far stronger than their representation in the Constituent Assembly.

Above all, the realities of power favored the Bolsheviks. They had full majorities in Petrograd and Moscow and their strength was great in other industrial centers. Their government had the positions of power in the cities and in the army, while the opposition's strength lay chiefly in the unorganized millions of peasants. Moreover, the Bolsheviks were united and determined, with a clearcut program which seemed to meet the needs of the people. The opposition was unorganized and lacked driving force.

Also, it was unable to offer an alternative to the program that the Bolsheviks were already carrying out.

The Attitude of the Bolsheviks. The Bolsheviks, realizing that the Constituent Assembly would become the focal center for all anti-Bolshevik elements, whether socialist or upper class, were determined not to permit it to play the counter-revolutionary role that the French National Assembly had played in 1848. On December 11, 1917, the Soviet government forcibly prevented an attempt of former ministers of the Provisional Government to convene the Assembly ahead of time. Shortly thereafter, Lenin wrote his "Theses on the Constituent Assembly," published in *Pravda* on December 26, 1917. Here he stated that a Constituent Assembly had been highly desirable after the fall of the Tsar, when the revolution was still in its moderate or "bourgeois" stage. Now, however, the revolution was in its socialist stage, with the Bolsheviks establishing the dictatorship of the proletariat and its allies, the poorer peasantry. As for the bourgeoisie, they were in open counter-revolution. Hence, any attempt to treat the Constituent Assembly from a purely theoretical, legalistic point of view was treason to the proletariat. Either the Assembly would declare its acceptance of the Soviet government and its program, or else the crisis that would result "can be solved only by revolutionary means."

In order to cut the ground from beneath the feet of the Constituent Assembly, it was decided to have the Third Congress of Soviets meet three days after the opening of the Assembly, and the Congress of Peasant Deputies a few days later. On January 16, the Central Executive Committee drafted a Declaration of Rights of the Toiling and Exploited People, for adoption by the Assembly. It opened with a declaration that Russia was a republic of Soviets, to which all power belonged, and a statement that it was a "free union of free nations, as a federation of national Soviet republics." There followed a long pronouncement for the Constituent Assembly to make, upholding Soviet policy and legislation. Finally, two paragraphs stated that, as the Constituent Assembly had been elected on the basis of party lists compiled before the changed situation after the fall of the Provisional Government, "it would be basically incorrect to set itself up against the Soviet power. . . ." Furthermore, the Assembly, supporting the Soviet regime, would recognize that its role was merely to be "the general working out of the fundamental principles of the socialist reconstruction of society."

The Dissolution of the Constituent Assembly. Lenin and his followers, then, had already made up their minds to deal rigorously with the Constituent Assembly unless it proved to be tame and toothless. Nevertheless, realizing that this body, advocated for decades by Russian liberals and revolutionaries, might enjoy immense prestige in the eyes of the populace, they did not want to shock public opinion by unnecessarily brutal treatment of it. It was permitted to meet, but the vicinity of the Tavrida Palace was surrounded by heavily armed troops, and the galleries were crowded with soldiers and sailors with rifles, pistols, and cartridge belts. For their part, the SR's had sought the support of some regiments, but as they refused to let them come out under arms, even those soldiers who sympathized with the moderates refused their appeal. A demonstration of civilian sympathizers with the Assembly —largely intellectuals and other white-collar workers— occurred, but it met the well-armed troops and was dispersed by gunfire, with some loss of life.

When the meeting opened, Sverdlov, a veteran Bolshevik, seized temporary control in order to read the Declaration of the Rights of the Toiling and Exploited People. After briefly urging the Assembly to adopt it, he withdrew to his seat. The big bloc of SR's now took over, electing Chernov as permanent chairman, in spite of Bolshevik warnings that they should support the program of active socialism. The session dragged on for almost twelve hours. At midnight the crucial vote was taken on the Bolshevik declaration, which lost, 237 to 138. Later, the Bolsheviks withdrew from the meeting, because of its "counter-revolutionary majority." The Left SR's withdrew an hour later. Not long before daybreak the sailor in command of the guard, apparently under orders from Lenin, asked that the meeting adjourn "because the guard is tired." There was a brief flurry of activity, during which a resolution on land and an appeal to the Allies for peace were read and declared approved. Neither of these differed greatly from the measures taken by the Second Congress of Soviets after the fall of the Kerensky government. Then, a little before five in the morning, the meeting adjourned until late afternoon.

The Constituent Assembly never met again. The Central Executive Committee, after a strong speech by Lenin, declared that it was dissolved, and an armed guard at the doors prevented it from reconvening. There was scarcely any protest against the dissolution: The Constituent Assembly had given no heroic leadership to the people and had failed to gain effective support. Probably if it had been convened six months before, the result would have been far different.

The Third Congress of Soviets. The Third Congress of Soviets met on January 23, 1918, and sought to step into the place of the Constituent Assembly. It promptly confirmed the dissolution of the latter, singing the *"Internationale"* with enthusiasm as a sign that the proletarian revolution was now victorious. Martov, one of the few Mensheviks present, objected that in a backward country like Russia the shift from a nonsocialist to a socialist society would be possible "only after prolonged work . . . to re-create a whole new political organization of society." Lenin's position on this point was (*see Reading No. 39*) that the war had caused Russia to mature with unusual speed, so that workers, soldiers, and peasants had decided: "we will take the whole power and will ourselves undertake the building of a new life." Hence, there could be no turning back to a bourgeois-democratic revolution.

Lenin's argument was in line with the political realities of the moment, but there still remained the difficult problem of building socialism and establishing the dictatorship of the proletariat in a country where the proletariat was both weak and uneducated. This problem was to cause much trouble in years to come.

— 10 —

CIVIL WAR AND WORLD WAR

Centers of Disaffection. While the new Soviet government was dealing with political and economic problems, a small-scale civil war was going on in the south and in the Urals. In Tiflis, the Georgian Mensheviks managed to hold out, as the Soviet arm was not yet long enough to reach to Georgia. In the other centers of disaffection, however—in the Don, Kuban, and Orenburg Cossack areas, and in the western Ukraine—the power of the government in Petrograd, weak as that power was, proved strong enough to overcome its foes for the time being. As for the war with Germany, victory here was out of the question. Lenin, who was determined to have peace, was forced to buy it at the cost of grievous sacrifices.

War in the Don Country. As General Kaledin of the Don Cossacks, like the Ukrainian *Rada,* was opposed to the Soviet regime, on December 13, 1917 Lenin sent Antonov-Ovseenko, the captor of the Winter Palace, to deal with Kaledin. Antonov's forces were weak and undisciplined bands of volunteer soldiers, sailors, and Red Guards, which were, however, strong enough to perform the allotted task. Against them were arrayed the Don Cossacks. They were more conservative than the ordinary peasants, thanks to their superior economic position and a long military tradition, but the war had severely shaken their conservative outlook. The Cossack regiments that returned from the front proved to be neutral or even hostile to the local regime of Kaledin and his officers. Moreover, living among the Cossacks were numbers of peasants, much poorer and hence more radical than the Cossacks. Like the peasants, the workers of the cities of Rostov and Taganrog were radical and strong in their support of the Soviet government. Hence, Kaledin's regime was faced with much local opposition, while its support from the Cossacks was far from solid.

The Volunteer Army. Fortunately for General Kaledin, General Alexeev, former chief-of-staff of the Russian army, had come to Rostov in mid-November to organize an anti-Bolshevik Volunteer Army. Although he managed to enroll a few fighters, funds and supplies were extremely scanty, and the dim prospects for success discouraged all but the most bitter and reckless of the officers. After Kornilov, Denikin, and three other generals made their way to Rostov in disguise, the Volunteer Army began to grow. It was composed almost entirely of officers from the former upper classes, most of them with grim scores to settle with the Bolsheviks, and during the first months it numbered only three or four thousand. Nevertheless, it proved strong enough to save the day for Kaledin on December 15, 1917, after the Military Revolutionary Committee of Rostov had driven the Don Cossacks from that city.

The Collapse of the Cossack Regimes. Even after this feat, Kaledin, who was trying to avoid open conflict with the Soviet government, remained cool to Alexeev's force. Kaledin even arranged for a new compromise Don Cossack government to be set up in January, 1918, in hopes that Antonov would halt his advance. But Antonov persisted, and the fatal hour for Kaledin was fast approaching. As Antonov's forces drew nearer, a Don Cossack Military Revolutionary Committee was set up late in January, and many of the Cossacks fought for the Soviets against Kaledin and their brethren. With this aid and with the support of the insurgent workers, the Reds defeated the Cossacks decisively. On February 11, Kaledin resigned his post as Ataman of the Don and shot himself.

Other Cossacks and the Volunteer Army fought on with the bravery of desperation, but the odds were too great. The Red Cossacks seized the Cossack capital on February 25, and all resistance there ceased. The Volunteer Army, which had been defending Rostov, fought its way out of a trap and retreated through terrible hardships toward the Kuban Cossack region. But here, too, the Soviets were in control, and the Volunteers, with a few Kuban Cossack recruits, had to take refuge in the wilds of the North Caucasus. All organized resistance to the Soviet power seemed to be at an end in the Don and the Kuban.

While these events were taking place on the Don, the

Orenburg Cossacks had been making a last stand in the Urals. For a considerable time they managed to hold off the Red Guards of Orenburg and other towns, but finally, on February 2, 1918, the Red forces took Orenburg. The remnants of the Orenburg Cossacks fled under Ataman Dutov.

The Struggle for the Ukraine. As has been said, the *Rada* had been set up in Kiev, claiming to speak for all the Ukraine. It had managed to take possession of Kiev early in November, after the local Soviet forces had driven off the supporters of the Provisional Government. The *Rada* was composed of Ukrainian nationalists, largely intellectuals, and supported to a considerable degree by the peasants of the Western Ukraine, who felt that they had more to gain from a government of their own countrymen in Kiev than from the new Russian government in faroff Petrograd. But the *Rada* never had much support from the urban workers, who were often Russian or Russified, nor from the large Jewish elements. In the eastern Ukraine, especially, the workers of the Donets Basin and other industrial centers gave strong support to the Soviets, and even the peasants of the eastern Ukraine did not appear to be greatly interested in the *Rada*.

From the beginning the relations between the *Rada* and Red Petrograd were strained. On December 17 the Soviet government, tired of negotiating, sent an ultimatum to the *Rada* demanding that it cease recalling Ukrainian troops from the army, that it stop disarming Soviet troops, and that it no longer permit troops and individuals to move across its territory to join Kaledin. The *Rada* was given forty-eight hours to avert war by satisfying these demands. The *Rada* replied that its actions were in keeping with its program of a federal union of peoples, based on self-determination, and claimed that the Soviet government was attempting to subjugate the Ukraine. For a time conflict was avoided, but all efforts at compromise came to nothing. Late in December, the Bolshevik leaders of Kiev fled to Kharkov, where they joined in the formation of a Ukrainian Soviet government. On December 29, 1917, this was recognized by the Russian Soviet government as the true government of the People's Ukrainian Republic.

The Fall of the *Rada*. In the ensuing conflict the troops of the *Rada* proved to be of little value. Although the *Rada* received its chief support from the Ukrainian peasants, its regiments, consisting largely of the peasantry, were easily won over by Bolshevik propaganda, which stressed the giving of all land to those who worked it. Muraviev, the Red commander, captured Poltava, his first objective, with losses of only one man killed and a few wounded. The Ukrainian nationalist forces proved so vulnerable to social agitation that they were unable to make a successful stand against Muraviev's forces, poor and weak though these were. As the Red forces approached, uprisings of workers eased the capture of one town after another. By the beginning of February, 1918, the Soviet army was approaching Kiev, where the *Rada* forces were hard put to it to suppress an uprising of workers. Although the revolt was suppressed, Muraviev pushed relentlessly on, and after several days of heavy bombardment and street-fighting, Kiev fell to the Reds on February 9. The *Rada* ministers fled to the western Ukraine. The Ukrainian Soviet government installed itself in Kiev.

Thus, in the Ukraine, as in the Cossack territories, the Soviet forces, small and undisciplined as they were, proved able to overcome their enemies and to establish the authority of the revolutionary regime. But in both the Don and the Ukraine the Red troops quickly antagonized many of the inhabitants by their lack of discipline and the lawless killings, looting, and other outrages, which continued unchecked in spite of the efforts of the local Soviets. Furthermore, the requisitioning of grain to supply troops and urban populations angered the peasants. When the German and Austrian troops entered these regions a few weeks later as a result of the peace treaty of March, 1918, the Soviet regimes were driven in disorder from the Ukraine and the Don.

Peace Negotiations with the Germans. In the summer and fall of 1917, perhaps the strongest argument of the Bolsheviks in winning support was the demand for peace. Lenin had consistently held that the war was an imperialistic conflict, in which the blood of the toiling peoples was shed for the selfish interests of the bourgeoisie. After the Provisional Government had fallen and the Soviet power had been established, Lenin's first act had been to propose an immediate peace to the warring governments and to the peoples, on whom he counted more than he did on the rulers. As neither peoples nor governments showed any signs of acting of the proposal, the Soviet government, on November 21, 1917, instructed General Dukhonin, the commander-in-chief, to begin negotiations with the Germans for an armistice. Two days later Lenin ordered the soldiers and sailors to begin fraternization with the enemy on all the fighting fronts.

At this time, Trotsky, Commissar for Foreign Affairs, officially notified the Allied ambassadors of the Soviet peace move. The neutral diplomats were also informed of the proposal, which they were asked to transmit to the enemy powers. The Allies completely refused to entertain this proposal, and, indeed, they counselled Dukhonin to refuse to seek an armistice—advice that helped to bring him to his untimely end. The Soviet peace overtures appeared to be fruitless.

But while the Allied governments floundered about, trying to decide what to do about this hated revolutionary government and the menacing proposal for a general armistice, three Soviet emissaries, on November 26, under a white flag, made contact with the German headquarters and requested an armistice. The German High Command proposed a meeting at Brest-Litovsk on December 2. Trotsky promptly invited the Allied powers to take part in the talks, but in vain. Hence, on December 2, the Soviet delegation, headed by the veteran Bolshevik A. A. Joffe, went alone to Brest-Litovsk. Here the plebeian members of the Soviet party, which included a peasant and a worker chosen at random, met with the aristocratic officers of the German army and the polished German diplomats. Actually, social differences played little part, as both sides wanted peace. Only the arrogant General von Hoffmann took pains to remind the Russians that they represented a defeated country. In spite of sharp disagreements about the German refusal to withdraw from the Baltic islands they had captured, and a Soviet proposal that the Germans promise not to transfer troops to the Western front, a compromise was reached that satisfied the Russians while leaving the Germans freedom to move the bulk of their troops. On December 5, the armistice was agreed on; the first peace negotiations were to be begin on December 22.

The Discussion of the Peace Terms. When the Soviet delegation returned to Brest to begin the peace negotiations, it was in a very weak bargaining position. The Russian army was worthless in battle, for the soldiers demanded peace at any price, as Lenin well knew. On the other hand, it was imperative to obtain the best possible terms from the victors, in order to avoid infuriating the many Russians who still had feelings of national pride. Above all, it was necessary to drag out the talks as long as possible in order to utilize them as a forum from which to influence world opinion. It was especially important that the German workers should perceive how ruthless and greedy their government was, so that the coming German revolution might be stimulated and advanced. Lenin, who like all the Bolshevik leaders, was convinced that the German revolution would surely come, was however, less hopeful that it would arrive on scheduled time than were most of his associates.

The representatives of the Central powers were in a much better bargaining position, although they, too, had weaknesses. Count Czernin, the Austrian Foreign Minister, was so convinced of his country's need for peace and bread at once that he was ready to sign with the Russians on almost any terms. Austria, however, was so dependent upon Germany that Czernin's frantic longing for peace had little effect upon the negotiations. Kühlmann, the German Foreign Minister, was less urgent in his need for peace, although he felt it advisable to show a conciliatory attitude. He seems to have had some faint hopes that a moderate policy in the East might induce the Allies to agree to peace talks, and also did not want to outrage the German socialists, who were becoming increasingly restive. General von Hoffmann, however, felt no such qualms. As representative of Ludendorff and the Supreme Command, he had every intention of using the German superiority over the Russians to best advantage, without bothering about the diplomatic niceties.

The Issue of Self-Determination. At the outset the Soviet peace proposal, which spelled out the principles of no annexations and no indemnities, was presented by Joffe. It included self-determination for Poland and other peoples who lacked freedom, and speedy withdrawal of troops from areas occupied during the war. These points,

which would have required the Germans to withdraw from
the Baltic and Polish territories they had conquered, were
not to the liking of any of the representatives of the
Central powers. But because Kühlmann and Czernin
wished to avoid too blatant an exhibition of Germany's
land-grabbing attitude, Kühlmann, on December 25, 1917,
made a very conciliatory reply, although he made the
reservation that Germany could agree to such renunciation only if all the warring powers agreed to observe
the same rules. General von Hoffmann, however, soon
dispelled some of the Soviet illusions by telling Joffe that
if some of the occupied territories (Poland and the Baltic
regions) decided to secede and ask annexation, Germany
would regard this as an example of self-determination.
This aroused great indignation among the Russian delegation, which talked of breaking off the negotiations, and
Count Czernin, in despair, even threatened to make a
separate peace with Russia. But Hoffmann, convinced that
Germany had the whip hand over both Russia and
Austria, refused to budge, and in the end the Russians
resumed the talks. After a tentative agreement was finally
reached, a ten-day interval was provided in order that the
Allies might be informed of the terms. This, however,
brought no response from the Western powers.

The Climax of the Peace Talks.   Nevertheless, when
the talks were resumed on January 9, 1918, the situation
had changed. Trotsky had replaced Joffe as head of the
Soviet delegation, imparting to it a more unyielding and
aggressive attitude. The Central powers, however, were
greatly heartened by the appearance of a Ukrainian delegation at Brest-Litovsk. As the *Rada* was already suffering
defeats at the hands of the Red forces, it was eager to
make peace with the Germans on almost any terms, which
opened to the Central powers the alluring prospect of
access to the rich supplies of grain and other foods from
the Ukraine. Trotsky, not realizing the nearness of the
collapse of the *Rada,* agreed that the Ukrainians might
take part in the negotiations.

For a time the renewed proceedings consisted of an
acrid debate between Kühlmann and Trotsky. The latter
repeatedly punctured the German claim that the desire of
the peoples of the occupied territories to unite with
Germany had been a real expression of popular will.

Kühlmann, claiming that the assemblies in Poland and the Baltic lands that had made the request were truly expressions of the wishes of the people, had considerable difficulty in parrying Trotsky's ironical thrusts and needed Hoffmann's blunt reminders that Germany was the victor in the East to redress the balance. Probably neither side hoped to persuade the other of the correctness of its claims. Trotsky undoubtedly was using the forum of Brest-Litovsk in an effort to delay matters until the German and Austrian revolutions, which were sputtering and giving off sparks, might burst into flame. Kühlmann also was in no hurry, as he wished a peace that was not too obviously imposed. Moreover, the negotiations with the *Rada* had not been completed.

The German Terms. Finally, even Kühlmann had had enough. On January 18, 1918, he had General von Hoffmann lay on the table a map with a blue line marking the boundary that the Germans proposed. It ran north from Brest-Litovsk to the Baltic, cutting off from Russia all of Poland, Lithuania, and western Latvia, including Riga and the Moon Islands. South of Brest-Litovsk the boundary would be worked out between the Germans and the *Rada* government. The line coincided almost exactly with the position of the German troops at the time. Hoffmann, in answer to an ironical question from Trotsky, stated frankly that it was based upon military considerations, and that it would give law and order to the people west of the line and a chance for self-determination. While no time limit was set for the acceptance of these terms, it was obvious that they were the last word of the Germans. Trotsky played for time with a proposal that the conference should recess for several days. While he may have hoped that the German revolution would come to the rescue, he also felt it necessary to confer with Lenin and the other Soviet leaders as to the proper course of action.

"No Peace, No War." When the German proposals were considered in Petrograd, three different proposals for dealing with them were offered. Lenin, backed by Zinoviev, Kamenev, and Stalin, felt it necessary to accept after all possible delay had been obtained. A group of Left extremists headed by Bukharin, however, urged rejection of the German offer and the proclaiming of a "revolutionary war." They hoped that this radical action would inflame the German workers and other revolutionary elements, who would be disillusioned if the Russians tamely signed. Trotsky took a middle position. He realized that a revolutionary war was out of the question, but, like Bukharin, he felt that Russia should not accept the German terms. Hence, he proposed a refusal to accept the German demands, accompanied by an announcement that Russia would unilaterally withdraw from the war and demobilize her armies. Lenin argued cogently against these proposals, pointing out that the Soviet regime needed months of peace to achieve stability. He agreed that the German revolution was on the way, but was doubtful that it would come in time to save the Russian revolution from the collapse that would result from further attempts to fight the Germans. But Bukharin's doctrine of "revolutionary war" seemed far more popular with the Bolshevik leaders. It took all of Lenin's cold realism to persuade the Bolshevik Central Committee to reject Bukharin's scheme and accept Trotsky's compromise of "no war, no peace," by a vote of nine to seven.

On January 30, Trotsky led his delegation back to Brest-Litovsk, accompanied by two representatives of the Ukrainian Republic, which at that moment was on the point of taking Kiev. But the Germans and the Austrians were not concerned over the defeats of the *Rada,* as they realized that a small force of German and Austrian troops could easily recapture Kiev and restore the *Rada* to power. Trotsky's sarcastic references to the helplessness of the *Rada* did not disconcert Kühlmann, who promised Hoffmann he would break off the talks as soon as the delegates of the *Rada* signed a treaty. For a time, however, Trotsky convinced Kühlmann that the Soviets would accept a more moderate proposal. But on February 10, after the *Rada* Ukrainians had signed a treaty very favorable to the Germans, the break came. Trotsky rejected the proposal for discussing more moderate terms of peace and in a ringing speech he brushed aside the possibility of making peace with one of the imperialistic camps. Russia would withdraw from the war and demobilize its army, without sanctioning "the conditions which German and Austro-Hungarian imperialism is writing with the sword upon the bodies of living peoples."

The German Reaction. The German leaders, momentarily confused by this unprecedented move, soon recovered. On February 13, the highest civil and military personnel of Germany conferred as to the proper course to take. It was decided to clear up the situation in the East by a quick stroke, in order to release troops for the Western front and to gain the grain supplies of the Ukraine. Thus, on February 18, the German army marched gaily forward. There were no refusals on the part of the German troops to fight revolutionary Russia. Moreover, as Lenin had predicted, the Russian army was completely incapable of defense. Ludendorff gleefully stated that it was enough to send a company of troops ahead by rail or motor to capture a town and disarm the Russians. The Germans rolled ahead, capturing a broad belt of territory and taking huge quantities of munitions, supplies, and prisoners.

As soon as the German advance was known, the Bolshevik Central Committee conferred on the crisis. Bitterly and with passion, Lenin castigated the policy of "playing with war," which would lead to the end of the revolution unless peace were made. The revolution would still endure even if Latvia, Estonia, and Finland were given up. Trotsky came over to Lenin's side, which provided a majority for immediate acceptance of the German terms. A radio message to that effect, signed by Lenin and Trotsky, was at once sent to Berlin. For three days no reply was received by the Soviet leaders, who undertook feverish preparations to delay and oppose the German advance. Eventually, however, after the German forces had reached their objectives (which did not include the capture of Petrograd and Moscow), new German terms were sent to the Soviet government on February 22.

The Signing of the Peace Treaty.   The new peace terms included the evacuation of all Latvia and Estonia, the signing of a peace between Soviet Russia and the Ukrainian *Rada* government, and the withdrawal of Russian forces from the Ukraine and Finland. Obviously, the Germans were planning to establish their control over these territories. The Soviet government was held to strict limits in accepting the proposals. It was granted two days to decide, three more days to come to Brest-Litovsk and sign the treaty, and two more weeks to ratify it.

At this point Lenin also proved uncompromising. Thoroughly weary of revolutionary phrase-making, he declared that since Russia had no army to fight a revolutionary war they must accept the German terms. Unless this was agreed to he would resign. This threat, which would have split the party disastrously, brought Trotsky and Dzerzhinsky to drop their opposition to signing. In addition, several members of the Central Committee abstained from voting on the issue, with the result that Lenin's proposal for accepting the onerous terms of the Germans was carried by a slim margin.

Trotsky's reluctance to approve signing was based largely upon hopes of Allied aid for a revived Russian resistance to Germany. While the various Allied ambassadors were all strongly hostile to the Soviet government, three unofficial Allied representatives—Colonel Raymond Robins of the American Red Cross, R. H. Bruce Lockhart of Britain, and Captain Jacques Sadoul of France—were hopeful of reviving the Russian army for further fighting against Germany. The Central Committee of the Communist party on February 22 had reluctantly approved a policy of accepting supplies and military instructors from the Allies. Lenin, who was not present for the voting, sent a scribbled note that he was "in favor of taking potatoes and arms from the bandits of Anglo-French imperialism." But, although Robins, Lockhart, and Sadoul were working feverishly to arrange some concrete measures of Allied support, it was still a very uncertain matter. Hence, Lenin, after winning a majority of his party's Central Committee, pressed the Central Executive Committee of the Soviet Government to approve the decision for peace. It proved a difficult matter to obtain a majority, but after an all-night session Lenin's relentless realism won out. As the victorious Bolsheviks left the hall there were shouts: "Traitors! Judases! German spies!" from the Left Socialist Revolutionaries.

On March 3, the Russian delegation signed the treaty at Brest-Litovsk. In order to indicate that it was a dictated rather than a negotiated peace they refused to discuss its terms, and Sokolnikov, who now was head of the delegation, stated that it was a treaty "which Russia, grinding its teeth, is compelled to accept." He asserted his confident belief, however, "that this triumph of the imperialist and the militarist over the international proletarian revolution is only a temporary and passing one."

Ratification of the Treaty. The final Treaty of Brest-Litovsk, which had been made even more burdensome than had been expected by the last-minute cession of important parts of Transcaucasia to the Turks, was extremely unpopular in Soviet Russia. The Left Socialist Revolutionaries detested it and withdrew from the Council of People's Commissars in protest. An active group of Left Bolsheviks, who had set up their own journal, *Kommunist,* furiously denounced the treaty. Even Lenin, although he was convinced of the necessity of ratifying it, waited until the last minute to see what the Allies would do. The three Allied agents were still working for Allied support for a Russian resumption of war against Germany. Lockhart, especially, was quite hopeful of obtaining British aid for a new Eastern front—a scheme which Trotsky was eagerly fostering. Lenin, although highly sceptical of aid from the Allies, put off the ratification of the treaty until the last minute in order to see if any concrete pledges of Allied aid would be made. Nevertheless, his main reliance was on the treaty, whose ratification he relentlessly pushed.

On March 6, a small Congress of the Bolshevik party was called to consider the treaty. Lenin again took the lead in insisting on its ratification, bringing out all his familiar arguments that Russia had no army to fight a revolutionary war. He reminded his audience that in 1807 Russia had signed the Treaty of Tilsit with Napoleon with the intention of breaking it as soon as it proved possible. This treaty, he added, they were already breaking. The Congress voted approval of the treaty by a vote of 28 to 12, with four abstentions. It also adopted a secret resolution calling for general military training in Russia and declaring that the Russian proletariat would throw all its resources into the work of supporting the "brotherly revolutionary movement of the proletariat of all countries." As these activities were directly counter to specific provisions of the treaty, the need for secrecy was obvious.

Final Ratification. The Left Communists continued to rage against the "obscene" policy of Lenin. They and the Left Socialist Revolutionaries exerted their full strength in opposition to the treaty when it was presented to the Fourth Congress of Soviets on March 14. Even Lenin was still ready to consider an alternative policy, for he postponed the meeting of the Congress from the 12th to the 14th in order to give Colonel Robins time to receive an expected pledge of American aid to Russia if the treaty were rejected. During the three days of debate most of the speakers opposed ratification.

Finally, when President Wilson sent merely a cordial message of sympathy instead of the firm pledge of aid that Robins had been awaiting, and no further word came from London or Washington, Lenin took the platform. In a calm, logical speech he presented his arguments for ratification. Further war with Germany was out of the question, he declared, leaving this grievous treaty the only thing possible. He termed it a Tilsit peace, which to his hearers carried the hope that sometime in the future the Russian people would undo this settlement as they had the one with Napoleon. When Lenin finished, the Congress voted, 784 to 261, for ratification, with 115 abstentions. Russia was at peace with the Central powers for the first time since August, 1914.

The Price of Peace. The terms of the treaty imposed by the Germans were extremely severe. (*See Reading No. 40.*) The territory lost included all of Russian Poland and the region out of which the states of Lithuania, Latvia, and Estonia were later formed. Furthermore, the Russians were compelled to withdraw completely from Finland, where a Leftist regime was fighting on fairly even terms against conservative Finnish forces. German troops landed in southwestern Finland, in the rear of the Reds, in April, 1918, with the result that the latter were completely routed by the German and White Finnish forces and a strongly conservative, anti-Soviet government was established, taking over the northern shore of the Gulf of Finland almost to Petrograd.

The treaty also compelled the Soviets to relinquish their position in the Ukraine, where the Soviet Ukrainian forces had recently occupied Kiev. With the help of German and Austrian forces, the weak Soviet troops were driven out, and German control, exerted nominally through weak Ukrainian regimes, was instituted. Even the region of the Don seemed to be lost to the Soviet state, for here General

Krasnov, liberally supplied with arms by the Germans, extended his power almost to the Volga at Tsaritsyn. The Turks received some small but highly important areas in the western Caucasus and later expanded their sway over much of Transcaucasia. In all, then, the treaty took away some 1,300,000 square miles of territory, with an estimated population of 62,000,000.

The effect of these losses upon the Russian economy was immense. Poland and the Baltic were not essential to the economic life of the country, but the Ukraine was a different story. Here was concentrated most of Russia's coal and iron production, as well as almost all the country's sugar factories. In all the areas occupied by the Central powers lay approximately half of Russia's industrial equipment, with a great part of it in the Ukraine. In the broad Ukrainian fields grew abundant crops of grain and other farm products, sorely needed by the starving Russian cities. Therefore, although Soviet Russia still embraced vast expanses stretching to the Arctic and the Pacific, the loss of the relatively small parts taken away had a disastrous effect upon the economic life of the country.

To make matters worse, in a supplementary treaty of August, 1918, the Soviet government had to agree to pay 6,000,000,000 marks in a series of installments "for losses caused to Germans by Russian measures." Indeed, it seems likely that if Germany had been able to win a smashing victory over the Western powers, the German leaders would have used their dominant position in the East to seek to impose full hegemony over the Soviet state.

Allied Wrath Against Soviet Russia. To the Allies it appeared that Russia was already a German satellite. German troops from the Eastern front streamed west in 1918, while substantial supplies of food from the Ukraine and other borderlands seized by the Germans did much to alleviate the starvation in Austria and Germany. The apparent subservience of the Soviets to the Germans aroused the bitter resentment of the Allies and gave a pretext for armed intervention in Russian affairs. Even before the signing of the Treaty of Brest-Litovsk, the British and the French had urged approval of a Japanese landing at Vladivostok, although the actual landing did not occur until April, 1918, after Wilson's opposition had been largely worn down. As more and more German troops from the Russian front were thrown into Ludendorff's last drives in France, the hostility of the Allies toward the Soviet leaders who had made this possible grew apace. It seems possible that the Allies might never have embarked upon more than two years of active intervention in Russia against the Communist regime if they had not been embittered by the Peace of Brest-Litovsk.

Domestic Effects.   Within Soviet Russia the political consequences of the peace were grave. Like the great majority of the Socialist Revolutionaries, those of the Left, who were allied with the Bolsheviks, were highly patriotic. They showed their intense displeasure with the treaty by resigning their seats in the Council of People's Commissars and, although they did not at once oppose Lenin and his followers, before many months the Left Socialist Revolutionaries rose in active revolt against the Soviet government. Doubtless many other Russians turned against Lenin and his party for their apparent subservience to Imperial Germany. The increasing food shortage that resulted in part from the loss of the rich Ukrainian fields to the Germans also made the Soviet regime more unpopular.

In spite of these unfavorable consequences of the peace, it none the less seems that Lenin had no choice but to accept the German terms. He had taken power largely on the basis of his pledge to make peace—a pledge which he immediately moved to carry out. Indeed, to fight any longer against the Germans was completely impossible, in view of the breakdown of the army. It appears probable that, in spite of the alienation of large numbers of people by the peace treaty, Lenin nevertheless gained support because of it, as the war was so thoroughly hated by great parts of the population. To many it was a wonderful thing to have the slaughter ended, bad though some of the aspects of the peace might be. Moreover, the peace gave the new Soviet government the inestimable benefit of a breathing-spell—a chance to organize the new administration, to consolidate its power, and to undertake the creation of a new army to replace the old Russian army. Brief though the period of grace proved to be, it is quite possible that if it had not been obtained the Soviet regime might have collapsed into anarchy and ruin.

— 11 —

CONCLUSION

Much of the history of the last half-century of the Russian empire centered around the popular struggle to obtain a more democratic regime and to ease the lot of the peasants. The government of the Tsar stubbornly fought against the liberal elements and failed to utilize favorable moments to deal with the basic problems. The First and Second Dumas, which, unrepresentative as they were, nevertheless spoke for the people, were prevented from dealing with the land problem, and the masses lost their power to express their will through legal channels. Conceivably Stolypin's land solution, although presented to the peasants without consultation of their will, might have solved the agrarian problem. But it was not given a proper trial.

Long before the twenty years had elapsed that Stolypin had thought necessary for success, a rash and adventurous foreign policy had plunged Russia into the disastrous war of 1914. In this conflict the backward governmental system, of which the rise of Rasputin to power was merely the most spectacular aspect, ensured defeat. The terrible blood bath in 1914 and 1915 occurred before he had gained control. The added losses of 1916 and the serious food shortage of the last months, which produced the final explosion, intensified but did not create the growing disgust with the calamitous war.

The Provisional Government of March, 1917, had a magnificent opportunity to set up a permanent democratic, liberal regime. It failed to do so, not because of too much democracy, but because of too little. The middle and upper classes, who throughout exerted great influence on the Provisional Government, consistently refused to permit land reform and to end the war on a compromise basis. An insincere and tricky foreign policy was aggravated by the unnecessary offensive of July, which resulted in disaster. The peasants were urged not to seize the land of the landowners but to wait for the Constituent Assembly to deal with the problem in a legal manner. At first this advice was heeded by the peasants, but as the Constituent Assembly was repeatedly postponed and the innocuous efforts of Chernov to prepare the basis for agrarian reform were made impossible, the peasants grew impatient. Finally, the strivings of the conservative elements to suppress the masses by setting up a military dictatorship under Kornilov aroused soldiers, workers, and peasants to anger. They felt that the government was still showing more sympathy for the upper classes than for the common people.

Kerensky, who headed the government that had repeatedly failed to satisfy the intense popular demands, perhaps could have saved the day by accepting the imaginative program of General Verkhovsky for a purely defensive war and for social reforms that would meet the needs of the masses. But Verkhovsky got short shrift, and the temporizing policy continued. Lenin and the Bolsheviks, who had already won the support of huge parts of the populace, had little difficulty in mobilizing overwhelming armed force to overthrow this government that had failed its vital tests.

Once it was in power, the new Soviet government, led by Lenin, acted with determination and vigor, in marked contrast to the Provisional Government. The peasants were gladdened by a law that turned all land over to them for use, and the government did all it could—albeit unsuccessfully—to improve the lot of the factory workers. The Constituent Assembly, which threatened to install in power the moderate elements that had failed to use their opportunities in the preceding months, was summarily dealt with in the name of the dictatorship of the proletariat. Passive resistance by the moderate political parties was scornfully disregarded, while the Cheka—the political police—was set up to deal with more violent opponents of the regime. Feeble armed resistance to the Soviet regime— in the Don, the Urals, and in the Ukraine—was easily suppressed, and the stability of the Soviet government was increased.

Finally, the thorny problem of peace with Germany was grasped firmly by Lenin. Although it required a rapid advance by the German army to secure acceptance of Lenin's counsel of accepting the harsh German terms, he almost single-handed persuaded the Bolshevik party and the Congress of Soviets to ratify the Treaty of Brest-Litovsk. Thus, the Soviet government obtained an end to the fighting, which permitted the consolidation of the regime's forces for the terrible struggles that were to come. The failures of the Provisional Government had given Lenin and the Bolsheviks their chance. Although far from infallible, they met and passed the first test.

The outstanding feature of the whole revolutionary period is the mistakes made by the elements in power. The Tsar and his supporters repeatedly failed to satisfy the basic demands of the masses for agrarian and political reform. Subsequently, the failings of the imperial regime were made vastly more obvious by its terrible mismanagement of the war, so that the indignation of the people rose to the boiling point.

After the Tsar had been overthrown, it was the turn of the Provisional Government to grapple with the nation's problems. It, too, failed repeatedly. Its insistence on prosecuting the war and its refusal to take any action on agrarian reform spelled its doom and made easy the path of the Bolsheviks. The latter were fortunate in having a leader of great skill, acuteness, and determination, who proved able to make the most of the opportunities offered. He did not make the opportunities, however; they had been made by his predecessors. Lenin's genius lay in profiting by the mistakes of others, and then in avoiding similar mistakes when he and his party had won power. But the basis of his power had been prepared by Nicholas II and Kerensky.

Part II

READINGS

— Reading No. 1 —

FAILINGS OF THE RUSSIAN ARMY MEDICAL SERVICE IN 1914[1]

In the fall of 1914, M. V. Rodzianko, Chairman of the Duma, heard disturbing reports of the lack of proper medical care for the wounded. After a visit to the front area he made the following observations.

After the first battles reports began to come from the front about the disturbing state of sanitary affairs in respect to the movement of the wounded. . . . The confusion was complete. Freight trains came to Moscow, in which the wounded lay without straw, often without clothing, badly bandaged, unfed for several days. At that time my wife, supervisor of the Elizabeth Society, received reports . . . that such trains were passing by their detachments and even were standing at the stations, and the nurses were not admitted to the trains and remained idle. . . .

Worst of all was the rendering of first aid by the military: there were neither wagons nor horses, nor first aid supplies, and moreover, other organizations were not allowed to go to the forward areas. . . .

Soon after my arrival at Warsaw in 1914 Vyrubov . . . came to me and proposed that we visit the Warsaw-Vienna station, where there were about 17,000 men wounded in the battles at Lodz and Berezini. At the station we found a terrible scene: on the platforms in dirt, filth, and cold, in

[1] From M. V. Rodzianko, "Krushenie Imperii," *Arkhiv Russkoi Revoliutsii* (Berlin, 1926), XVII, 82-85, translated by J. S. Curtiss.

the rain, on the ground, even without straw, an unbelievable quantity of wounded, who filled the air with heart-rending cries, dolefully asked: "For God's sake, order them to dress our wounds, for five days we have not been attended to." It must be said that after the bloody battles these wounded had been hauled in complete disorder in freight cars and abandoned at the Warsaw-Vienna station without aid. The only medical forces that attended these unfortunates were Warsaw doctors, aided by volunteer nurses. . . .

— Reading No. 2 —

CONTINUED SHORTAGES OF MUNITIONS IN 1915 [2]

The lack of ammunition and even rifles continued extreme during the desperate fighting of 1915. The Tsar mentioned it to the Empress in his letter of July 7 from Headquarters.

✓   ✓   ✓

. . . Again that cursed question of shortage of artillery and rifle ammunition—it stands in the way of an energetic advance. If we should have three days of serious fighting we might run out of ammunition altogether. Without new rifles, it is impossible to fill up the gaps. The army is now almost stronger than in peace time; it should be (and was at the beginning) three times as strong. This is the situation in which we find ourselves at present.

If we had a rest from fighting for about a month our

[2] *Perepiska Nikolaia i Aleksandry Romanovykh,* III, 241, as quoted in Frank Alfred Golder, *Documents of Russian History* (New York, 1927), p. 193. Quoted by permission of Appleton-Century-Crofts, Inc.

condition would greatly improve. It is understood, of course, that what I say is strictly for you only. Please do not say a word of this to anyone.

— Reading No. 3 —

THE OPPOSITION OF THE EMPRESS AND RASPUTIN TO THE REFORM MOVEMENT [3]

In the summer of 1915, the pressure of public opinion forced the Tsar to remove some of the worst of the ministers, and to replace them with able and respected men like A. A. Polivanov, Minister of War. In September, however, Nicholas, urged by the Empress, defied the Duma and his ministers by going to Headquarters and taking command of the army. The Empress remained as his deputy in charge of political matters. She, in turn, was strongly under the influence of Gregory Rasputin ("our Friend"), and at his bidding she secured the removal of the respectable ministers and filled the cabinet with disreputable figures like B. V. Stürmer and A. D. Protopopov, who were willing to collaborate with Rasputin. These developments are vividly shown in the strange phrasing of the Empress' letters to the Tsar.

1   1   1

September 2nd 1915
Now the *members of the Duma* want to meet in Moscow to talk over everything when their work here is

[3] From *Letters of the Tsaritsa to the Tsar 1914-1916* (New York, 1924), pp. 130, 135, 221, 260, 287, 289-290, 297, 382, 395, 411, 412, 428-429, 439, 442, 453-454, 455-456.

closed—one ought energetically to forbid it, it will only cause great *troubles*.—If they do that—one ought to say, that the *Duma* will then not be reopened till much later —threaten them, as they try to the ministers—& the gouvernement. Moscow will be worse than here, one must be severe—oh, could not one hang *Gutchkov?*

Nov. 15-th 1915

Now, before I forget, I must give you over a message from our Friend, prompted by what He saw in the night. He begs you to order that one should advance near Riga, says it is necessary, otherwise the Germans will settle down so firmly through all the winter, that it will cost endless bloodshed and trouble to make them move—now it will take them so aback, that we shall succeed in making them retrace their steps—he says this is just now the most essential thing and begs you seriously to order ours to advance, he says we can and we must, and I was to write it to you at once.—

Jan. 7-th 1916

Lovy, I don't know, but I should still think of Stürmer, his head is plenty fresh enough—. . . Stürmer would do for a bit, & then later on if you ever want to find another you can change him. . . . He very much values *Gregory* wh. is a great thing.

Jan. 9-th 1916

Oh, how I wish you could get rid of *Polivanov,* wh. means *Gutchkov*—old Ivanov in his stead, if honest Beliaev too weak—. . . .

March 4-th 1916

Remember about Polivanov. . . .

March 12-th 1916

Maklakov . . . entreats to see me also beseeching that I shld. implore you quickly to get rid of *Polivanov*, that he is simply a revolutionist under the wing of *Gutchkov*— Stürmer begged the same. . . . *Maklakov* says . . . quickly clear out *Polivanov*, any honest man better than him.

Aug. 8-th 1916

. . . Our Friend hopes we won't climb over the Carpathans and try to take them, as he repeats the losses will be too great again.

Sept. 9-th 1916

. . . Please, take Protopopov as minister of the Interior, as he is one of the *Duma*, it will make a great effect amongst them & shut their mouths.—

Sept. 14-th 1916

Yesterday had *Stürmer* & spoke alright—I begged him quickly to change Obolensky, otherwise we may have great disorders in the streets (on account of food) & he will at once loose his head & all are against him. God bless yr. new choice of *Protopopov*—our Friend says you have done a very wise act in naming him.—

Sept. 23-rd 1916

Our Friend says about the new orders you gave to *Brussilov* etc.: "*Very satisfied with father's orders, all will be well.*" He won't mention it to a soul, but I had to ask His blessing for yr. decision.—

Oct. 30-th 1916

Forgive me for what I have done—but I had to—our Friend said that it was absolutely necessary. *Protopopov* is in despair he gave you that paper the other day, thought he was acting rightly until *Gr.* told him it was quite wrong. So I spoke to *Stürmer* yesterday & they both completely believe in our Friend's wonderful, God sent wisdom. *St.* sends you by this messenger a new paper to sign giving over the whole *food supply* now at once to the minister of Interior. *St.* begs you to sign it & at once return it, . . . then it will come in time before the *Duma* assembles on Tuesday. I had to take this step upon myself as *Gr.* says *Protop.* will have all in his hands & finish up all the *Unions* & by that will save Russia. . . .

It will be a rotten *Duma*—but one must not fear—if too vile, one closes it. Its war with them & we must be firm.— Tell me, you are not angry—but those men listen to me & when guided by our Friend—it must be right—they, *Pr.* & *St.* bow before His Wisdom.

Nov. 11.th

. . . Forgive me, deary, believe me—I entreat you dont go and change *Protopopov* now, he will be alright, give him the chance to get the *food supply matter* into his hands & I assure you, all will go. . . .

Dec. 13.th 1916

. . . He [Rasputin] entreats you to be firm, to be the Master & not always to give in to *Trepov*—you know much better than that man (still let him lead you) & why not our Friend who leads through God. Remember why I am disliked—shows it right to be firm & feared & you be the same, you a man,—only believe more in our Friend (instead of *Trepov*). He lives for you and Russia. And we must give a strong country to Baby, & dare not be weak for his sake, else he will have a yet harder reign, setting our faults to right & drawing the reins in tightly which you let loose. . . .

Its all getting calmer & better, only one wants to feel

Your hand—how long, years, people have told me the same—"Russia wants to feel the whip"—its their nature—tender love and then the iron hand to punish & guide.

                              Dec. 14.th 1916

If you hear fr. *Kalinin* again & he begs to close the *Duma*—do it, don't stick to the 17.th—time is money, the moment golden, & if dawdled over difficult, impossible to catch up & mend again. . . . Be Peter the Great, John the Terrible, Emperor Paul—crush them all under you—now don't you laugh, naughty one—but I long to see you so with all those men who try to govern you. . . .

. . . Disperse the Duma at once. . . . I should have quietly & with a clear conscience before the whole of Russia have sent *Lvov* to Siberia (one did so for far less grave acts), . . . *Miliukov, Gutchkov* & *Polivanov* also to Siberia. It is war and at such a time interior war is high treason, why don't you look at it like that, I really cannot understand.

— Reading No. 4 —

FORMATION OF THE
PETROGRAD SOVIET [4]

By March 12, the leaders of the insurrection had begun to organize a Soviet in Petrograd to supply guidance for the popular uprising. The following were its first publications:

              ✓   ✓   ✓

[4] From *Izvestiia of Committee of Petrograd Journalists*, No. 1, March 12, 1917, as quoted in Frank Alfred Golder, *Documents of Russian History* (New York, 1927), pp. 285-286. Quoted by permission of Appleton-Century-Crofts, Inc.

During the day [March 12, 1917] representatives of workers and soldiers and several public leaders assembled at the building of the State Duma. A Soviet of Workers' Deputies was organized, which resolved to issue a call to the people.

The Soviet of Workers' Deputies resolved to address the following proclamations to the inhabitants:

I

CITIZENS: The representatives of the workers, soldiers, and inhabitants of Petrograd, meeting in the State Duma, announce that the first session of their representatives will take place at seven o'clock tonight in the building of the State Duma. All those troops that have joined the side of the people should immediately elect their representatives, one for each company. Factory workers should elect one deputy for each thousand. Factories with less than one thousand workers should elect one deputy each.

THE PROVISIONAL EXECUTIVE COMMITTEE
OF THE SOVIET OF WORKERS' DEPUTIES

II

CITIZENS: The soldiers who have joined the side of the people have been in the streets since morning without food. The Soviet of Deputies, workers, soldiers, and inhabitants are making every effort to feed the soldiers. But it is hard to organize the food supply at once. The Soviet appeals to you, citizens, to feed the soldiers as best you can.

THE PROVISIONAL EXECUTIVE COMMITTEE
OF THE SOVIET OF WORKERS' DEPUTIES

— Reading No. 5 —

THE PROCLAMATION OF THE PROVISIONAL GOVERNMENT AND ITS PROGRAM[5]

After the revolution had won Petrograd, the leaders of the Duma, who had taken no part in it, decided to set up a Provisional Government to save the country from falling into anarchy. Its members were the leading figures of the former Progressive Bloc.

✔   ✔   ✔

Citizens, the Provisional Executive Committee of the members of the Duma, with the aid and support of the garrison of the capital and its inhabitants, has triumphed over the dark forces of the Old Regime to such an extent as to enable it to organize a more stable executive power. With this idea in mind, the Provisional Committee has appointed as ministers of the first Cabinet representing the public, men whose past political and public life assures them the confidence of the country.

Prince George E. Lvov, *Prime Minister and Minister of the Interior*

P. N. Miliukov, *Minister of Foreign Affairs*

A. I. Guchkov, *Minister of War and Marine*

M. I. Tereshchenko, *Minister of Finance*

A. A. Manuilov, *Minister of Education*

A. I. Shingarev, *Minister of Agriculture*

N. V. Nekrasov, *Minister of Transportation*

A. I. Konovalov, *Minister of Commerce and Industry*

A. F. Kerensky, *Minister of Justice*

Vl. Lvov, *Holy Synod*

[5] *Izvestiia,* No. 4, March 16, 1917, as quoted in Frank Alfred Golder, *Documents of Russian History* (New York, 1927), pp. 308-309. Quoted by permission of Appleton-Century-Crofts, Inc.

The Cabinet will be guided in its actions by the following principles:

1. An immediate general amnesty for all political and religious offenses, including terrorist acts, military revolts, agrarian offenses, etc.

2. Freedom of speech and press; freedom to form labor unions and to strike. These political liberties should be extended to the army in so far as war conditions permit.

3. The abolition of all social, religious and national restrictions.

4. Immediate preparation for the calling of a Constituent Assembly, elected by universal and secret vote, which shall determine the form of government and draw up the Constitution for the country.

5. In place of the police, to organize a national militia with elective officers, and subject to the local self-governing body.

6. Elections to be carried out on the basis of universal, direct, equal, and secret suffrage.

7. The troops that have taken part in the revolutionary movement shall not be disarmed or removed from Petrograd.

8. On duty and in war service, strict military discipline should be maintained, but when off duty, soldiers shall have the same public rights as are enjoyed by other citizens.

The Provisional Government wishes to add that it has no intention of taking advantage of the existence of war conditions to delay the realization of the above-mentioned measures of reform.

President of the Duma, M. Rodzianko
President of the Council of Ministers, Prince Lvov
Ministers Miliukov, Nekrasov, Manuilov, Konovalov, Tereshchenko, Vl. Lvov, Shingarev, Kerensky.

— Reading No. 6 —

RESOLUTIONS OF THE PEASANTS' UNION[6]

In April a large gathering of peasants from all parts of Russia adopted resolutions strongly urging peace without conquests and asking that all the land be given to those who tilled it.

✓   ✓   ✓

1. The meeting of the Peasants' Union . . . on April 8, 1917, in which three thousand citizens, peasants, and soldiers participated, resolved:

That it is necessary to go ahead with the war for freedom, but that the Russian people has no need of conquests; that the Russian people, after freeing the areas ruined by the belligerents, needs a peace in the interest of the laboring classes of the world. Having taken into consideration the call of the Soviet of Workers' and Soldiers' Deputies to the people of the world, a call which guarantees liberty and self-determination to all peoples and opposes new conquests, the meeting greets the Minister of Justice, Kerensky, and empowers him to defend before the Provisional Government questions of war and peace and to strive to persuade the Provisional Government to renounce, at once, all aims of conquest.

1. The meeting of the Peasants' Union thinks that the Russian people, having thrown off the yoke of the autocracy, desires neither a limited nor an unlimited tsarist government, but a democratic republic.

2. The meeting of the Peasants' Union believes that the land should be handed over to the workers, and that each

[6] *Izvestiia,* No. 27, April 11, 1917, as quoted in Frank Alfred Golder, *Documents of Russian History, 1914-1917* (New York, 1927), pp. 373-374. Quoted by permission of Appleton-Century-Crofts, Inc.

person who tills the soil with his own hands has the right to the use of it.

3. The meeting greets the Soviet of Workers' and Soldiers' Deputies and all Socialist parties . . . in their fight for land and freedom.

4. To make it possible at once to plant the idle fields no matter to whom they belong.

— Reading No. 7 —

THE PETROGRAD SOVIET APPEALS FOR PEACE TO THE PEOPLES OF THE WORLD [7]

On March 27, 1917, the Petrograd Soviet, composed chiefly of moderate socialists, issued an appeal to the peoples of the world to compel their governments to make a just peace.

✔   ✔   ✔

Comrade-proletarians, and toilers of all countries:

We, Russian workers and soldiers, united in the Petrograd Soviet of Workers' and Soldiers' Deputies, send you warmest greetings and announce the great event. The Russian democracy has shattered in the dust the age-long despotism of the Tsar and enters your family as an equal, and as a mighty force in the struggle for our common liberation. Our victory is a great victory for the freedom and democracy of the world. The chief pillar of reaction

[7] *Izvestiia,* No. 15, March 28, 1917, as quoted in Frank Alfred Golder, *Documents of Russian History, 1914-1917* (New York, 1927), pp. 325-326. Quoted by permission of Appleton-Century-Crofts, Inc.

in the world, the "Gendarme of Europe," is no more. May the earth turn to heavy granite on his grave! Long live freedom! Long live the international solidarity of the proletariat, and its struggle for final victory! . . .

Conscious of its revolutionary power, the Russian democracy announces that it will, by every means, resist the policy of conquest of its ruling classes, and it calls upon the peoples of Europe for concerted, decisive action in favor of peace.

We are appealing to our brother-proletarians of the Austro-German coalition, and first of all, to the German proletariat. . . .

We will firmly defend our own liberty from all reactionary attempts from within, as well as from without. The Russian revolution will not retreat before the bayonets of conquerors, and will not allow itself to be crushed by foreign military force. But we are calling to you: Throw off the yoke of your semi-autocratic rule, as the Russian people have shaken off the Tsar's autocracy; refuse to serve as an instrument of conquest and violence in the hands of kings, landowners, and bankers—and then by our united efforts, we will stop the horrible butchery, which is disgracing humanity and is beclouding the great days of the birth of Russian freedom.

Toilers of all countries: we hold out to you the hand of brotherhood across the mountains of our brothers' corpses, across rivers of innocent blood and tears, over the smoking ruins of cities and villages, over the wreckage of the treasuries of civilization;—we appeal to you for the reestablishment and strengthening of international unity. In it is the pledge of our future victories and the complete liberation of humanity.

Proletarians of all countries, unite!

PETROGRAD SOVIET OF WORKERS' AND
SOLDIERS' DEPUTIES

— Reading No. 8 —

LENIN'S APRIL THESES [8]

On April 17, Lenin, who had just returned from Switzerland, addressed a Bolshevik meeting, where he set forth his April Theses, urging an uncompromising radical program toward the war, the land, and the Provisional Government. This account, drawn from notes by a participant at the meeting, is fragmentary, but it gives a clear statement of Lenin's drastic proposals.

Lenin's Speech at a Caucus of the Bolshevik Members of the All-Russian Conference of the Soviets of Workers' and Soldiers' Deputies, April 17, 1917.

I have outlined a few theses which I shall supply with some commentaries. I could not, because of the lack of time, present a thorough, systematic report.

The basic question is our attitude toward the war. The basic things confronting one as he reads about Russia or observes conditions here are the triumph of defensism, the triumph of the traitors to Socialism, the deception of the masses by the bourgeoisie. . . . The new government, like the preceding one, is imperialistic, despite the promise of a republic—it is imperialistic through and through.

1. In our attitude toward the war not the slightest concession must be made to "revolutionary defensism," for under the new government of Lvov & Co., owing to the capitalist nature of this government, the war on Russia's part remains a predatory imperialist war. . . .

In view of the undoubted honesty of the mass of rank and file representatives of revolutionary defensism who accept the war only as a necessity and not as a means of

[8] From V. I. Lenin, *Collected Works,* Vol. XX, Book I (New York, 1929), pp. 95-102. Quoted by permission of International Publishers.

conquest, in view of their being deceived by the bourgeoisie, it is necessary most thoroughly, persistently, patiently to explain to them their error, to explain the inseparable connection between capital and the imperialist war, to prove that without the overthrow of capital it is *impossible* to conclude the war with a really democratic, nonoppressive peace.

This view is to be widely propagated among the army units in the field. . . .

2. The peculiarity of the present situation in Russia is that it represents a *transition* from the first stage of the revolution, which, because of the inadequate organization and insufficient class-consciousness of the proletariat, led to the assumption of power by the bourgeoisie—to its second stage which is to place power in the hands of the proletariat and the poorest strata of the peasantry. . . .

This peculiar situation demands of us an ability to adapt ourselves to the specific conditions of party work amidst vast masses of the proletariat just wakened to political life.

3. No support to the Provisional Government; exposure of the utter falsity of all its promises, particularly those relating to the renunciation of annexations. Unmasking, instead of admitting, the illusion-breeding "demand" that *this* government, a government of capitalists, cease being imperialistic. . . .

4. Recognition of the fact that in most of the Soviets of Workers' Deputies our party constitutes a minority, and a small one at that, in the face of the *bloc* of all the petty-bourgeois opportunist elements . . . who have yielded to the influence of the bourgeoisie. . . .

It must be explained to the masses that the Soviet of Workers' Deputies is the only possible form of revolutionary government and that, therefore, our task is, while this government is submitting to the influence of the bourgeoisie, to present a patient, systematic, and persistent analysis of its errors and tactics, an analysis especially adapted to the practical needs of the masses. . . .

5. Not a parliamentary republic—a return to it from the Soviet of Workers' Deputies would be a step backward—but a republic of Soviets of Workers', Agricultural Laborers' and Peasants' Deputies throughout the land, from top to bottom.

Abolition of the police, the army, the bureaucracy. . . .

All officers to be elected and to be subject to recall at any time, their salaries not to exceed the average wage of a competent worker. . . .

6. In the agrarian program, the emphasis must be shifted to the Soviets of Agricultural Laborers' Deputies.

Confiscation of private lands.

Nationalization of all lands in the country, and management of such lands by local Soviets of Agricultural Laborers' and Peasants' Deputies. A separate organization of Soviets of Deputies of the poorest peasants. Creation of model agricultural establishments out of large estates . . .

7. Immediate merger of all the banks in the country into one general national bank, over which the Soviet of Workers' Deputies should have control . . .

8. Not the "introduction" of Socialism as an immediate task, but the immediate placing of the Soviet of Workers' Deputies in control of social production and distribution of goods . . .

9. Party tasks:
   A. Immediate calling of a party convention.
   B. Changing the party program, mainly:
      1. Concerning imperialism and the imperialist war.
      2. Concerning our attitude toward the state, and our demand for a "commune state."
      3. Amending our antiquated minimum program.

10. Rebuilding the International.

Taking the initiative in the creation of a revolutionary International, an International against the social-chauvinists and against the "center" . . .

— Reading No. 9 —

MILIUKOV'S NOTE ON WAR AIMS[9]

On May 1, 1917, Foreign Minister Miliukov sent a note to the various Allied governments denying that the new Russian government was seeking a separate peace. Declaring that the new Russia was more than ever inspired by the lofty democratic aims of the Allies, he continued:

Imbued with this spirit of a free democracy, the declaration of the Provisional Government cannot, of course, afford the least excuse for the assumption that the revolution has entailed any slackening on the part of Russia in the common struggle of the Allies. Quite to the contrary, the aspiration of the entire nation to carry the world war to a decisive victory has grown more powerful, thanks to our understanding of our common responsibility, shared by each and every one. This striving has become still more active, since it is concentrated upon a task which touches all and is urgent—the task of driving out the enemy who has invaded our country. It is obvious . . . that the Provisional Government, while safeguarding the rights of our own country, will, in every way, observe the obligations assumed toward our Allies.

Continuing to cherish the firm conviction of the victorious issue of the present war, in full accord with our Allies, the Provisional Government feels also absolutely certain that the problems which have been raised by this war will be solved in a spirit that will afford a firm basis for lasting peace, and that the leading democracies, in-

[9] From *Riech,* No. 91, May 3, 1917, as quoted in Frank Alfred Golder, *Documents of Russian History, 1914-1917* (New York, 1927), pp. 333-334. Quoted by permission of Appleton-Century-Crofts, Inc.

spired by identical desires, will find the means to obtain those guarantees and sanctions which are indispensable for the prevention of sanguinary conflicts in the future.

— Reading No. 10 —

LENIN'S ATTACK ON MILIUKOV'S NOTE[10]

In a furious article in Pravda, *Lenin on May 4 declared that Miliukov's note proved the predatory capitalist nature of the Provisional Government.*

✓   ✓   ✓

The cards are on the table. We have good reason to be grateful to Messrs. Guchkov and Miliukov for their note appearing in today's papers.

The majority of the Executive Committee of the Soviet of Workers' and Soldiers' Deputies, . . . all those who advocated confidence in the Provisional Government, are sufficiently punished. They hoped, expected, and believed that the Provisional Government . . . would forever repudiate annexations. It turned out differently. . . .

In its note . . . the Provisional Government announces the "striving of all the people(!) to carry on the war *to a decisive victory.*" "It is self-evident," adds the note, "that the Provisional Government . . . will fully meet our obligations to our Allies."

Short and clear. War to a decisive victory. The alliance with the English and the French bankers has been declared sacred. . . .

Who has concluded this alliance with "our" allies, *i.e.,*

[10] From V. I. Lenin, *Collected Works,* Vol. XX, Book I (New York, 1929), pp. 234-235. Quoted by permission of International Publishers.

with the Anglo-French billionaires? The Tsar, Rasputin, the Tsar's gang, of course. To Miliukov and Co., however, the treaty is sacred.

Why?

Some people say: Because Miliukov is insincere, is a trickster, etc.

But this is not the point. The point is that Guchkov, Miliukov, Tereshchenko, Konovalov represent the capitalists. And the capitalists need the seizure of foreign lands. They will get new markets, new places for the export of capital, new profitable jobs for tens of thousands of their sons, etc. The point is that at the present moment the interests of the Russian capitalists are identical with those of the English and the French capitalists. This, and this only, is the reason why the Tsar's treaties with the Anglo-French capitalists are so dear to the hearts of the Provisional Government of the Russian capitalists. . . .

The note of the Provisional Government squarely places before us the question: What next?

From the very first moment of our revolution, the English and French capitalists have been persuading us that the Russian Revolution was made for the one and only purpose, to continue the war "to the end." The capitalists are intent on robbing Turkey, Persia, China. If, in order to accomplish this purpose, it be necessary to slaughter another ten millions or so of Russian muzhiks,—why worry? As long as we get a "decisive victory." . . . Now the Provisional Government has frankly adopted the same view.

Fight—because we want the spoils.

Die, tens of thousands of you every day,—because "we" have not yet fought the thing to a finish, because we have not yet received our share of the loot! . . .

No class-conscious worker, no class-conscious soldier will further support the policy of "confidence" in the Provisional Government. The policy of confidence is bankrupt. . . .

Workers and Soldiers, declare openly: We demand that there be only one power—the Soviet of Workers' and Soldiers' Deputies. The Provisional Government, the government of a handful of capitalists, must give way to the Soviets.

— Reading No. 11 —

MILIUKOV'S EXPLANATION OF HIS FOREIGN POLICY[11]

Miliukov was soon driven from office because of his foreign policy. In a speech to his party on May 22, 1917, however, he made no apology for it, but to the contrary, gloried in it.

✓   ✓   ✓

At the present time I am not a member of the Provisional Government, but a free citizen and can, therefore, permit myself . . . to talk straight . . .

I admit quite frankly, and stand firmly by it, that the main thread of my policy was to get the Straits for Russia. I fought, unfortunately in vain, against those who favored the new formula [no annexations and no indemnities, and the right of self-determination], and that Russia should free the Allies from their obligations to help her secure sovereign rights over the Straits. I would say, and say it proudly, and regard it as a distinct service to the country, that until the last moment that I was in office, I did nothing which gave the Allies the right to say that Russia has renounced the Straits.

[11] From *Riech*, No. 109, May 24, 1917, as quoted in Golder, *op. cit.*, p. 334. Quoted by permission of Appleton-Century-Crofts, Inc.

— Reading No. 12 —

THE APPEAL OF THE SOVIET TO THE ARMY [12]

The Soviet, dominated by moderate Socialists, appealed on May 15, 1917, to the army to defend Russia by continuing to fight, even though the war had been caused by the rulers and capitalists.

✓   ✓   ✓

Comrade-Soldiers at the Front!

A heavy burden has fallen to your lot. With the price of your blood you have paid for the criminal act of the Tsar, who has sent you to fight and has provided you with neither guns, ammunition, nor bread. The working class did not need the war; they did not start the conflict. The tsars and the capitalists of all countries are responsible. For the people, every additional day of war is one more day of sorrow . . .

The Soviet of Workers' and Soldiers' Deputies has appealed to all peoples to bring the war to an end. It has appealed to the French, Germans, and Austrians. Russia awaits the answer to this appeal . . .

Remember, comrade-soldiers, that our appeal would be worthless if the regiments of William should crush revolutionary Russia before our fellow workmen and the peasants of other countries respond to our appeal. . . . What would happen if we should make a separate peace, if the Russian army should today stick its bayonets into the ground and say that it did not wish to fight any more, that it was not concerned with what happened to the rest of the world? This is what would happen: after crushing our

[12] From *Izvestiia,* No. 55, May 15, 1917, as quoted in Frank Alfred Golder, *Documents of Russian History, 1914-1917* (New York, 1927), pp. 397-399. Quoted by permission of Appleton-Century-Crofts, Inc.

Allies on the West, German imperialism would turn on us with all its might; the German Emperor, the German landholders and capitalists would . . . seize our cities, villages and land; they would lay a tribute on our people. Did we overthrow Nicholas so as to fall at the feet of William?

Comrade-soldiers! The Soviet calls you to peace by another way. It leads you to peace by appealing to the revolutionary workers and peasants of Germany and Austria to rise; it leads you to peace by the promise of our Government to give up the policy of conquest and to demand that the Allied powers do likewise . . .

But remember, comrade-soldiers, that this time will never come if you do not hold the enemy at the front . . . Remember that at the front, in the trenches, you are standing guard over Russian freedom. You are defending not the Tsar, Protopopov, Rasputin, wealthy landowners and capitalists, but the Russian Revolution, your brother workers and peasants.

Having sworn to protect Russian liberty, do not refuse to take the offensive if the war situation should demand it. The freedom and happiness of Russia are in your hands.

In defending this freedom, beware of provocation; beware of traps. The fraternization which is now developing at the front can easily become a trap . . . Not through fraternization, not through silent and separate understandings concluded at the front by individual companies, battalions, and regiments, will you get peace. Not in separate peace, not in separate truces, is the salvation of the revolution and the peace of the world. Those who tell you that fraternization is the way to peace, are leading both you and Russian freedom to destruction.

— Reading No. 13 —

TSERETELLI'S SPEECH AT THE CONGRESS OF SOVIETS [13]

At the first Congress of Soviets in June, 1917, the Menshevik H. G. Tseretelli, Minister in the Provisional Government, made a long speech praising the government's policies. To the surprise of most of those present, Lenin interrupted Tseretelli to announce the readiness of the Bolsheviks to take power.

In taking upon itself the fight for universal peace, the Russian revolution has also to take over the war, begun by other governments . . .

In order that it may succeed in its object, the Provisional Government must say clearly and emphatically . . . that it has broken with the old imperialist policy, and must propose to the Allies that the first question . . . is to re-examine on a new basis all agreements made until now . . . We should do nothing that would break our ties with the Allies . . . The worst thing that could happen to us would be a separate peace. It would be ruinous for the Russian revolution, ruinous for international democracy . . . Should we bring about a situation that would break relations with the Allies and necessitate a separate peace, the Russian revolution would be obliged, immediately afterwards, to take up arms on the side of the German coalition . . . Even if we brush aside the talk of a possible attack by Japan . . . can there be any doubt that the German coalition, continuing the war, would force the weaker side to give military support? . . .

[13] From *Izvestiia*, No. 84, June 19, 1917, as quoted in Frank Alfred Golder, *Documents of Russian History, 1914-1917* (New York, 1927), pp. 361-363. Quoted by permission of Appleton-Century-Crofts, Inc.

We come to the question of taking the offensive . . .
It is said that due to pressure from the imperialist circles,
the Provisional Government, and the Minister of War in
particular, are taking steps to bring about immediate action at the front, in order thereby to put an end to the
political campaign for universal peace . . . We believe
that the measures taken by Comrade Kerensky tend to
strengthen the cause of the revolution . . . It is clear to
us that now, when our country is threatened from the outside, the Russian revolutionary army should be strong,
able to take the offensive . . . Comrades, this inactivity
which has been going on at the front does not strengthen,
but weakens and disorganizes our revolution and
army . . .

As to the land question—we regard it as our duty at
the present time to prepare the ground for a just solution
of that problem by the Constituent Assembly. We believe
that the question of the passing of the land into the hands
of the laboring classes can and should be definitely settled
by the Constituent Assembly . . .

At the present moment, there is not a political party in
Russia which would say: Hand the power over to us,
resign, and we will take your place. Such a party does not
exist in Russia. (Lenin: "It does exist.") . . . They [the
Bolsheviks] say: When we have a majority, or when the
majority comes over to our point of view, then the power
should be seized. Comrade Lenin, you said that. At least
the Bolsheviks and you with them say it in their official
statements.

Gentlemen, until now, there has not been a single party
in Russia which has come out openly for getting itself all
power at once, although there have been such cries by ir-
responsible groups on the Right and the Left . . . The
Right says, let the Left run the Government, and we and
the country will draw our conclusions; and the Left says,
let the Right take hold, and we and the country will draw
our conclusions . . . Each side hopes that the other will
make such a failure, that the country will turn to it for
leadership.

But, gentlemen, this is not the time for that kind of a
play . . . In order to solve the problems of the country,
we must unite our strength and must have a strong Government, . . . strong enough to put an end to experi-

ments dangerous for the fate of the revolution, . . . experiments that may lead to civil war . . .

This, gentlemen, is our policy . . .

— Reading No. 14 —

RESOLUTIONS ADOPTED BY THE ALL-RUSSIAN CONGRESS OF SOVIETS[14]

When the First Congress of Soviets met in Petrograd on June 16, 1917, it was predominantly composed of moderate socialists, with the Bolsheviks in the minority. The resolutions of the Congress were moderate in character, voicing approval of the policy of the Provisional Government.

✓   ✓   ✓

The Congress . . . agrees that:

1. . . . it would have been a severe blow to the revolution to have handed over the power to the bourgeoisie alone; and

2. That it would have greatly weakened and threatened the revolution to have handed over all the power, at this time, to the Soviets of Workers' and Soldiers' Deputies, for such an act would have alienated certain elements of the population that are still able to serve the cause of the revolution.

For these reasons, the All-Russian Congress of Soviets of Workers' and Soldiers' Deputies approves the action of the Petrograd Soviet during May 3 and 4, in forming

[14] From *Izvestiia*, No. 87, June 22, 1917, as quoted in Frank Alfred Golder, *Documents of Russian History, 1914-1917* (New York, 1927), pp. 368-370. Quoted by permission of Appleton-Century-Crofts, Inc.

a coalition government on a definite democratic platform, both in foreign and domestic affairs.

Having heard the explanations of the comrade-ministers on the general policy of the Provisional Revolutionary Government, and having expressed full confidence in them, the All-Russian Congress agrees that this policy answers the interests of the revolution.

The Congress calls on the provisional Government to carry out resolutely and systematically the democratic platform which has been adopted, and in particular

a. To strive persistently for the earliest conclusion of a general peace without annexation, indemnity, and on the basis of self-determination;

b. To continue further the democratization of the army, and to increase its fighting power; . . .

g. Particularly does the Congress demand the speediest convocation of the All-Russian Constituent Assembly . . .

The Congress calls on all the revolutionary democracy of Russia to gather around the Soviets of Workers' and Soldiers' and Peasant Deputies, and to support the Provisional Government energetically in all its efforts to strengthen and broaden the conquests of the revolution.

This resolution . . . was accepted by a vote of 543 to 126 (52 not voting) . . .

— Reading No. 15 —

KERENSKY ORDERS THE ARMY TO TAKE THE OFFENSIVE [15]

On July 1, 1917, after intensive efforts to restore the morale of the troops, Kerensky, the Minister of War, ordered the army to take the offensive against the Germans and the Austrians.

Russia, having thrown off the chains of slavery, has firmly resolved to defend, at all costs, its rights, honor, and freedom. Believing in the brotherhood of mankind, the Russian democracy appealed most earnestly to all the belligerent countries to stop the war and conclude a peace honorable to all. In answer to our fraternal appeal, the enemy has called on us to play the traitor. Austria and Germany have offered us a separate peace and tried to hoodwink us by fraternization, while they threw all their forces against our Allies, with the idea that after destroying them, they would turn on us. Now that he is convinced that Russia is not going to be fooled, the enemy threatens us and is concentrating his forces on our front.

WARRIORS, OUR COUNTRY IS IN DANGER! Liberty and revolution are threatened. The time has come for the army to do its duty. Your Commander-in-Chief, beloved through victory, is convinced that each day of delay merely helps the enemy, and that only by an immediate and determined blow can we disrupt his plans. Therefore, in full realization of my great responsibility to the country, and in the name of its free people and its Provisional Government, I call upon the armies, strength-

[15] From *Izvestiia*, No. 96, July 3, 1917, as quoted in Frank Alfred Golder, *Documents of Russian History, 1914-1917* (New York, 1927), pp. 426-427. Quoted by permission of Appleton-Century-Crofts, Inc.

ened by the vigor and spirit of the revolution, to take the offensive.

Let not the enemy celebrate prematurely his victory over us! Let all nations know that when we talk of peace, it is not because we are weak! Let all know that liberty has increased our might.

Officers and soldiers! Know that all Russia gives you its blessing on your undertaking, in the name of liberty, the glorious future of the country, and an enduring and honorable peace.

Forward!

KERENSKY
Minister of War and Navy

— Reading No. 16 —

THE BREAKDOWN OF THE RUSSIAN OFFENSIVE [16]

After initial successes, Kerensky's July offensive bogged down and, when German reenforcements were thrown in, the retreat of the Russian army became a rout. The following telegrams from the Southwestern Front indicate the magnitude of the disaster.

The German offensive which began on July 19 at the front of the XI Army is turning into an unheard-of disaster, threatening the very existence of revolutionary Russia. The troops which have recently been brought up to the fighting line were influenced largely by the heroic

[16] From *Riech,* Nos. 160 and 161, July 24 and 25, 1917, as quoted in Frank Alfred Golder, *Documents of Russian History, 1914-1917* (New York, 1927), pp. 428-429. Quoted by permission of Appleton-Century-Crofts, Inc.

efforts of a small number of conscientious soldiers, but the enthusiasm of the offensive was quickly exhausted. The majority of the troops are becoming more and more demoralized. No one listens to authority or orders. Persuasion and pleading are in vain, and are answered by threats and even by shots. In some cases the men deserted their posts at the first shot of the enemy, and in other cases they did not even wait for the enemy to show himself. In some instances military units deserted in a body. Orders for hurried reinforcements were debated for hours at a meeting, and were carried out a day late. For a distance of a hundred versts [about 65 miles] in the rear one can see deserters on the move, with or without guns, able-bodied, bold, shameless, and fearless of consequences. Commissars and members of the army committees at the front are unanimously agreed that the situation calls for extreme measures and efforts, and that we should stop at nothing to save the revolution. Today the Commander of the XI Army, with the consent of the commissars and committees, gave orders to shoot at every one who runs from his post. Let the country know all the truth of what is going on here; let it tremble with rage, and let it find the determination to punish unmercifully the cowards who ruin and betray Russia and the revolution.

Signed by the commissars and chairman of the army committees at the front

I, Boris Savinkov, former commissar of the VII Army, and my assistant, Vladimir Gobechia, brought up the VII Army to a point of taking the offensive. The heroes fell in battle, and the army, carried away by their bravery, fought courageously; but now that they are no more, the army is on the run. How can I answer for the blood that is shed if I do not demand that order and discipline be enforced at once with an iron hand, so that cowards may not with impunity leave their posts, open the front, and by so doing sacrifice their comrades, faithful to their duty, and bring disgrace on Russia and the revolution? There is no choice. Death punishment to those who refuse to risk their lives for their country, for land and liberty.

Savinkov and Gobechia,
Commissar and Assistant Commissar of the Southwest Front

— Reading No. 17 —

AN APPEAL OF THE SOVIETS TO THE WORKERS AND SOLDIERS [17]

Popular dissatisfaction against the Government continued to mount in Petrograd during the first part of July, culminating in the enormous armed demonstration known as the July Days (July 16-18). Although the demonstrators demanded "All Power to the Soviets," the Soviets, led by moderate socialists, refused to take power and roundly condemned the demonstration as a threat to the revolution.

Comrade Workers and Soldiers:

Yesterday several Ministers, belonging to the Cadet Party, resigned. In view of this, there was a joint meeting of the Executive Committees of the All-Russian Soviets of Workers', Soldiers', and Peasants' Deputies, the fully authorized organs of the revolutionary democracy of all Russia, to act in the crisis. But this work was interrupted, notwithstanding the repeated warnings of the Soviet of Workers', Soldiers', and Peasants' Deputies.

Certain units of the army came out on the streets with arms in their hands, in an attempt to get control of the city. They seized automobiles, arrested individuals, and acted in a threatening manner. At the Taurida palace, they demanded that the Executive Committee should take all power. Having offered power to the Soviets, they were the first to encroach upon it. The All-Russian Executive organs of the Soviets indignantly refuse to yield to force.

[17] From *Izvestiia*, No. 109, July 18, 1917, as quoted in Frank Alfred Golder, *Documents of Russian History, 1914-1917* (New York, 1927), pp. 454-455. Quoted by permission of Appleton-Century-Crofts, Inc.

It is outrageous that a part of the garrison in one city should attempt to force its will on the whole of Russia.

On those who dared to call out an armed uprising lies the blood that was shed on the streets of Petrograd. It is a betrayal of our revolutionary army, which is defending the revolution at the front. He who stirs up trouble in the rear against the organs of democracy and brings about civil war in its ranks, is sticking a dagger in the back of the revolutionary army which is fighting the soldiers of William.

The All-Russian organs of the Soviets protest against these evil signs of undermining popular government, even the Constituent Assembly. The All-Russian organs of the Soviet demand that these shameful uprisings in revolutionary Petrograd be put to an end, once and for all. The Executive Committees of the All-Russian Soviets of Workers', Soldiers', and Peasants' Deputies call on all those who stand guard over the revolution and its conquests to await the decision of the fully empowered organs of democracy on this governmental crisis. All those to whom the cause of freedom is dear will accept the decision as the voice of all revolutionary Russia.

EXECUTIVE COMMITTEES OF ALL-RUSSIAN SOVIET OF WORKERS' AND SOLDIERS' DEPUTIES AND SOVIET OF PEASANTS' DEPUTIES

— Reading No. 18 —

THE CRISIS OF THE JULY DAYS[18]

In spite of the appeal of the Soviets, the July demonstrations took place, with masses of armed participants invading the Soviets. N. N. Sukhanov, a member of the

[18] From N. N. Sukhanov, *Zapiski o Revoliutsii* (Berlin, 1922), IV, 430-431, translated by J. S. Curtiss.

Petrograd Soviet, reports one such incident, when an armed worker demanded of the unwilling moderate socialists of the Soviets that they take power.

✐   ✐   ✐

I returned to the meeting. There was nothing new there. But now, like an arrow, there sped the news: the Putilov workers have arrived, numbering 30,000, they conduct themselves in extremely aggressive fashion, part of them have broken into the palace, they are seeking and demand Tseretelli . . . Tseretelli at that moment was not in the hall. It was said that they ran after him all through the palace, but they did not find him, he was not visible. In the hall disturbance, uproar, unrestrained shouts. At that moment a crowd of workers came storming in, numbering about forty men, many with rifles. The deputies jumped from their seats. Some of them do not display proper courage and self-control.

One of the workers, a classic *sans-culotte,* in a cap and a short blue shirt without a belt, with rifle in hand leaps up on the speaker's tribune. He trembles with emotion and rage and, brandishing his rifle, loudly shouts disconnected words:

"Comrades! Should we workers longer tolerate treachery? You have gathered here, you deliberate, you make deals with the bourgeoisie and landowners . . . You are busying yourselves with betrayal of the working class. Then know that the working class will not put up with it! There are 30,000 of us Putilovites here, to the last man! We'll get our way! Let there be no bourgeoisie! All power to the Soviets! The rifles are firm in our hands! Your Kerenskys and Tseretellis won't bamboozle us!"

Chkheidze, before whose nose the rifle was dancing, displayed restraint and full self-possession. In response to the hysterics of the *sans-culotte,* who was pouring forth his cold proletarian soul, the chairman, quietly bowing from his eminence, reached forth and inserted into the trembling hand of the worker the proclamation of the day before . . . :

"Here, comrade, take this, please, I ask you, and read it. Here it is stated what you and your Putilovite comrades should do. Please, read it and do not disrupt our sessions. Everything is stated there that is necessary . . ."

In the proclamation it stated that all those who had come out into the streets should head for home, otherwise they would be traitors to the revolution. The ruling Soviet group had nothing else to its name and Chkheidze found nothing else to present to the representatives of the proletarian depths at the moment of extreme intensity of their revolutionary will.

The *sans-culotte,* who had lost control of himself, not knowing what he should do next, took the proclamation and without difficulty was urged from the tribune. Soon they "convinced" his comrades to leave the hall. Order was reestablished, the incident was closed . . . But to this very moment the *sans-culotte* stands before my eyes on the tribune of the "White Hall," in self-oblivion shaking his rifle before the faces of the hostile "leaders of the democracy," in torment trying to express the will, yearning, and wrath of the true lower levels of the proletariat, who sensed betrayal but were powerless to combat it. This was one of the most beautiful scenes of the revolution. And in combination with the gesture of Chkheidze, one of the most dramatic.

— Reading No. 19 —

THE MOSCOW STATE CONFERENCE [19]

After the July Days the Provisional Government remained weak, as the masses of workers and soldiers still leaned toward the Bolsheviks. The conservative elements, apparently fearing the masses and distrustful of Kerensky

[19] From *Izvestiia,* No. 144, Aug. 28, 1917, as quoted in Frank Alfred Golder, *Documents of Russian History, 1914-1917* (New York, 1927), pp. 493-495. Quoted by permission of Appleton-Century-Crofts, Inc.

*and the Soviet, began to hope for a military dictator in
the person of the new Commander-in-Chief, General L. G.
Kornilov. The deep cleavage between the conservatives
and the moderate socialists became evident at the Moscow
State Conference (August 25-27, 1917), a gathering called
by Kerensky to lend support to the government.*

↑   ↑   ↑

The Bolshoi Theater was today definitely divided into
two parts—bourgeois and democratic . . . At 11:30 A.M.
the theater began to fill up. The delegates . . . all agreed
on one thing—there can be no peace between the different
groups . . .

At 11:15 A.M. General Kornilov drove up and was
given a triumphal reception. Flowers were showered upon
him, until his automobile was filled with them . . . At
11:50 he walked into the hall. As soon as he showed himself, the audience began to clap, and when he entered the
box where Generals Alexeev and Kaledin were seated he
was given a long and noisy ovation . . . He was cheered
by members of the Dumas, by the representatives of commerce and industry, by all the bourgeois groups and representatives of officers. But the delegates of the soldiers
committees sat quietly, without applauding. When, however, a few moments later, Kerensky with his ministers
appeared on the stage, the left side of the theater had its
revenge and gave Kerensky an ovation that lasted more
than five minutes. This time the right was motionless. Motionless, also, were the representatives of the officers and
the generals in their box.

The applause died down to break out with renewed
strength a second later. Shouts were heard, "Long live
Kerensky; long live the Provisional Government." Again
the noise subsided; again some one cried out, "Long live
the revolution"; and again the house was in an uproar. But
the right sat through it with hands folded, as if it did not
concern them . . .

General Kornilov took the floor . . . There is no doubt
that a certain part of the conference is expecting great
results from the General's speech. Some invisible hand has
pasted all over the city, posters with the General's por-
trait and biographical sketch. It cannot be said that the
General's speech justified the expectations of the right. It

gave many facts, but it could hardly be construed as the
speech of the future military dictator. It was more like
the speech of a general of a republic.

When Kornilov stepped forward, the right gave him a
long and noisy ovation, but the left and the soldiers sat
still. Shouts were heard: "Stand up, soldiers," but the
soldiers never budged . . . Kerensky added to the noise
by calling "Please come to order and listen to the first
soldier of the army, with the attention due him." . . .

[After Kornilov's speech, which stressed reviving the
discipline of the army, a number of other speakers followed, among them the Cossack General Kaledin.]

In his speech Kaledin, without any attempt to soften or
to mince words, presented the point of view and the hopes
of the so-called counter-revolutionists.

He said that he spoke in the name of the twelve
Cossack divisions, and protested against the accusation
that the Cossacks are counter-revolutionists . . . He continued by declaring, in a firm voice, that the soviets and
army committees must be done away with . . . These
words were greeted with applause from the right and by
shouts of "Never; we will not allow it," from the left.

Kaledin went on and said that there should be soldier
committees, but their functions should be limited to the
question of supplies. The declaration of the rights of
soldiers should be revised and supplemented with a declaration of the obligations of the soldiers. Discipline
should be reestablished; the former disciplinary punishment must be brought back.

The proposition was greeted by applause from the right
and by shouts of "counter-revolution" from the left, from
the representatives of the soldiers' committees.

Kaledin's speech made a deep impression, especially
the direct and uncompromising manner in which he
expressed himself. He emphasized each of his points with
the exclamation, "The Cossacks demand," etc. The Cossacks demand the dismissal of the soviets, the call of the
Constituent Assembly to Moscow . . . Kaledin finished
his speech amidst great applause from the right and
shouts of protest from the left.

As if to counter-balance Kaledin, the united democracy
put forward Chkheidze, chairman of the Central Executive
Committee of the Soviet of Workers' and Soldiers' Depu-

ties. His appearance was the signal for a stormy ovation, accompanied by the cries, "Long live the Soviet of Workers' and Soldiers' Deputies. . . ."

— Reading No. 20 —

GENERAL KORNILOV'S PROCLAMATION [20]

After the Moscow State Conference, General Kornilov, backed by many of the landowners, industrialists, army officers, and other conservatives, sought to seize the government. When he was unable to persuade Kerensky to surrender power, Kornilov sent a force of troops to seize Petrograd and overthrow the government. He issued the following appeal to the people.

People of Russia, our great country is dying. Her end is near.

Forced to speak openly, I, General Kornilov, declare that the Provisional Government, under the pressure of the Bolshevik majority in the Soviets, is acting in complete harmony with the German General Staff and . . . is killing the army and shaking the country.

The terrible conviction of the inevitable ruin of the country compels me in these frightful times to call upon all Russians to save their dying land. All in whose breast a Russian heart beats, all who believe in God, in the Church, pray to Him for the greatest miracle—the saving of our native land.

[20] From *Novoe Vremia*, No. 14866, Sept. 11, 1917, as quoted in Frank Alfred Golder, *Documents of Russian History, 1914-1917* (New York, 1927), pp. 521-522. Quoted by permission of Appleton-Century-Crofts, Inc.

I, General Kornilov, son of a Cossack peasant, declare to one and all that I desire nothing for myself other than the salvation of our Great Russia, and vow to lead the people, through victory over our enemies, to the Constituent Assembly, where it can determine its future destiny and the form of its future political life.

I cannot betray Russia into the hands of her ancient enemy, the Germans, who would make slaves of the Russian people. I prefer to die honorably on the field of battle so that I may not see the shame and degradation of our Russian land.

People of Russia, the life of your native land is in your hands.

GENERAL KORNILOV

— Reading No. 21 —

THE BREAKDOWN OF MILITARY DISCIPLINE [21]

The following reports from the Petrograd Telegraph Agency in the fall of 1917 show the complete collapse of discipline among the troops of the rear.

✓   ✓   ✓

Helsingfors, September 14. Last night . . . four officers of the . . . Petropavlovsk were shot by the sailors

[21] From A. L. Popov, *Oktiabrskii Perevot: Fakty i Dokumenty* (Petrograd, 1918), pp. 85-88, as quoted in James Bunyan and H. H. Fisher, *The Bolshevik Revolution, 1917-1918; Documents and Materials* (Stanford, 1918), pp. 29-31. Reprinted with the permission of the author and of the publishers, Stanford University Press. Copyright 1934 by the Board of Trustees of Leland Stanford Junior University.

. . . The officers refused to give a pledge of loyalty to the Provisional Government . . . In Vyborg a mob of soldiers removed from the guardhouse three generals and one colonel, who had been kept there by the . . . army committees . . . for alleged participation in the Kornilov affair, and threw them from a bridge into the water . . . After that a number of other regimental commanders and officers were attacked and thrown into the water. Those who tried to save themselves were killed. In all, about fifteen officers were killed . . .

Elisavetgrad, September 21 . . . A bloody encounter took place between a group of cadets and soldiers . . . One cadet, one soldier, and three unknown persons were killed; twenty-one wounded . . . The cadets were arrested. At the jail the soldiers attempted to lynch the cadets. One cadet committed suicide . . .

Army Headquarters, October 11. Headquarters received official news of the circumstances under which the departure of Generals Denikin, Elsner, Markov, and others took place from Berdichev . . . A mob of soldiers surrounded the building . . . where the generals were kept and demanded that the prisoners go to the station on foot. To avoid complications the soldiers' demand was satisfied, but to safeguard the prisoners the Commander-in-Chief of the Southwestern Front . . . walked all the way to the station beside the prisoners . . . At the station the soldiers demanded that the generals be placed in a prisoners' car instead of a second-class railway car. As no prisoners' car was available, a freight car had to be used instead . . .

Active Army, October 5. On October 3 a group of soldiers . . . destroyed the courthouse in the city of Dubno after a jury had condemned one of the instigators of a recent disturbance. Violence was done to the members of the jury and the court . . .

Irkutsk, October 5. [In view of recent disorders which took place in the city numerous arrests were made among the soldiers of the local garrison.] Yesterday morning . . . regiments of sharpshooters led by their agitators removed the rifles from the arsenal and refused to obey their commanders. The army commander, Lieutenant Krakovetsky, . . . was placed under arrest . . . A detachment which remained loyal to the revolution succeeded . . . in rescuing the commander . . . The rebels were disarmed . . .

Headquarters, October 11. Official reports were received here of the disorders which took place in the Letichevsky Uezd . . . In the village of Markovtsy a wine distillery was stormed and then set on fire . . . In Brailovka the soldiers plundered an estate and broke into a liquor cellar. Drunken soldiers are rioting and shooting at their fellow soldiers who were placed on guard of the liquor cellars. . . . In . . . Podolsk Gubernia soldiers are making unwarranted seizures of bread, fodder, horses, and oxen from large estates . . . No consideration is given to the property of manual workers . . .

Saratov, October 13 . . . In Balashev the local garrison rebelled and seized the post and telegraph. Soldiers travelling on the Riazan-Uralsk railroad are engaged in violent seizure of flour and other supplies.

— Reading No. 22 —

THE CONDITION OF THE TROOPS AT THE FRONT [22]

The troops at the front were no more dependable than those in the rear. An army intelligence report for October 2-13, 1917 paints a dismal picture of the morale of the frontline troops.

✓   ✓   ✓

Northern front. The situation in the army has not changed and may be described as a complete lack of con-

[22] From Belevsky Papers, Hoover War Library, Stanford University, as quoted in Bunyan and Fisher, *op. cit.,* pp. 24-26. Reprinted with the permission of the author and of the publishers, Stanford University Press. Copyright 1934 by the Board of Trustees of Leland Stanford Junior University.

fidence in the officers and the higher commanding personnel. The belief is growing among the soldiers that they cannot be punished for what they do . . . The influence of Bolshevik ideas is spreading very rapidly. To this must be added a general weariness, an irritability, and a desire for peace at any price.

Any attempt on the part of the officers to regulate the life of the army . . . is looked upon by the soldiers as counter-revolution . . . and stigmatized as a "Kornilov" move. The soldiers seem to believe that the arrest of Kornilov made void all the orders which he issued reinstating discipline. The army committees are in most cases helpless to guide the mob and are often compelled to follow it so as not to lose completely the confidence of the masses . . .

12th Army . . . The press of the political parties is no longer influencing the soldier masses. Again and again one hears the orders of the Provisional Government severely criticized. The committee of the 95th Regiment . . . declared Kerensky a traitor . . .

Apart from the Bolshevik not a single [political] movement has any popularity. Those who read moderate newspapers are looked upon as "bourgeoisie" and "counter-revolutionists." An intensive agitation is being conducted in favor of immediate cessation of military operations on all fronts . . .

Western front . . . Because of general war weariness, bad nourishment, mistrust of officers, etc., there has developed an intense defeatist agitation accompanied by refusals to carry out orders, threats to the commanding personnel, and attempts to fraternize with Germans. Everywhere one hears voices calling for immediate peace, because, they say, no one will stay in the trenches during the winter . . .

Among the phenomena indicative of tendencies in the life in the rear of the Western front are the recent disturbances at the replacement depot in Gomel. On October 1 over eight thousand soldiers who were to be transferred to the front demanded to be sent home instead . . . Incited by agitators they stormed the armory, took some fifteen hundred suits of winter equipment, and assaulted the Assistant Commissar and a member of the front committee. Similar events . . . have taken place in Smolensk . . .

Southwestern front . . . Defeatist agitation is increasing and the disintegration of the army is in full swing. The Bolshevik wave is growing steadily, owing to general disintegration in the rear, the absence of strong power, and the lack of supplies and equipment. The dominant theme of conversation is peace at any price and under any condition. Every order, no matter what its source, is met with hostility . . . Even their former leaders . . . —the committees—have lost their confidence . . . The commissars testify that the soldiers have lost all elementary notions of right, justice, and human worth. The position of the commanding personnel is very difficult. There have been instances of officers committing suicide . . .

The guard-cavalry corps of the 2d Army passed a resolution of no confidence in the majority of the officers. The soldiers are engaging in organized armed invasions of the surrounding country estates, plundering provisions, . . . of which there is a scarcity in the army. Not a thing can be done to counteract this restlessness, . . . as there is no force which could be relied upon in an attempt to enforce order. The activity of the courts is paralyzed because of the hostile attitude of the soldiers . . .

— Reading No. 23 —

THE RISING TIDE OF AGRARIAN DISTURBANCES [23]

While the military disorders and food riots increased in the fall of 1917, the peasants were rising to attack the es-

[23] From A. L. Popov, *Oktiabrskii Perevot,* pp. 81-83, as quoted in Bunyan and Fisher, *op. cit.,* pp. 31-33. Reprinted with the permission of the author and of the publishers, Stanford University Press. Copyright 1934 by the Board of Trustees of Leland Stanford Junior University.

*tates of the landowners. The following telegraphic reports
are typical of this period.*

⌁   ⌁   ⌁

Tambov, September 27. Accurate information about the
disorders in Kozlov Uezd has not been received up to the
present time. It is definitely known that one estate has
been pillaged and twenty-five have been burned. Besides,
many peasants living on separate farms all have suffered. . . .

Saratov, October 10. The agrarian disturbances in Ser-
dobsky Uezd embrace a large district. Peasants are stealing
cattle, dividing the land and forests, and carrying off the
grain. The uezd officials appealed for the aid of troops.
. . . The disorder has spread to Atkarsky Uezd.

Kishinev, October 10. Peasants of Megura village, Belet-
sky Uezd, influenced by propaganda, began to divide
among themselves the land and pastures of the neighboring estates of Borchel and Slobodzei.

Odessa, October 12. Word has been received of the
alarming situation in Akkerman and Orgeev, and also of
the increased agitation of the ignorant elements in Bere-
zovka. In Sorokovevsky Uezd agrarian disturbances continue. . . .

Voronezh, October 20. In Zadonsky Uezd . . . the
estates of Chertkov and other landowners have been par-
tially destroyed by the peasants. More than 60,000 puds
[1080 tons] of wheat and other grain have been burned.
Valuable old furniture has been destroyed. . . .

Zhitomir, October 23. After returning from a journey
to Volhynia the assistant commissar gave a report on the
situation. According to him, Volhynia is in a state of
complete anarchy. In many uezds there is general destruction of the forests and seizure of privately owned land. In
Staro-Konstantinovsky Uezd the Bolsheviks have seized
power. . . .

Penza, October 26. In Novocherkassk Uezd eight estates have been destroyed. Cavalry has been sent to stop
the disorder. In Krasnoslobodsky Uezd the estate of
Madame Lebedev and in Insarsky Uezd the estate of
Andronov have been pillaged.

Spassk, October 27. A wave of destruction swept over
the whole uezd. Felling and stealing of trees is going on.

The estate of Shreder has been pillaged and set on fire. The estate of Count Grabbe has been destroyed, including his valuable library.

Nizhni-Novgorod, November 1. According to the latest information the uprising has spread over six uezds, in which many estates have been pillaged and burned. The greatest disorder took place in Lukianovsky Uezd, where, according to the commissar, everything valuable is being ruthlessly destroyed. . . .

— Reading No. 24 —

FOOD RIOTS AND POGROMS[24]

After the Kornilov affair, the situation deteriorated steadily. The growing shortage of food produced the riots and disturbances portrayed in the following messages of the Petrograd Telegraph Agency.

Zhitomir, September 15. As a result of the rise in the price of bread a tumult has arisen among the women. In view of the prevailing agitation, troops and a detachment of Cossacks were called out. . . .

Simferopol, October 13. From a number of rural communities of Melitopolsky and Dneprovsky uezds comes information that shops are being wrecked and unauthorized searches are in progress. The uezd and gubernia

[24] From A. L. Popov, *Oktiabrskii Perevot,* pp. 72-79, as quoted in Bunyan and Fisher, *op. cit.,* pp. 29-31. Reprinted with the permission of the author and of the publishers, Stanford University Press. Copyright 1934 by the Board of Trustees of Leland Stanford Junior University.

commissars have been sent there and troops will be dispatched. . . .

Rostov-on-Don, October 10. In Azov, as a result of the dissatisfaction of the population with the rise in the price of bread and flour, disorder broke out. A crowd of residents marched to the city hall, broke into the food department, and attacked the government employees, who fled. When a member of the municipal government, Makarovsky, attempted to quiet the crowd, he was thrown down the stairs from the second floor, after which books, orders, and papers which were found in the department were flung about. Members of the Soviet of Workers' and Soldiers' Deputies who arrived at the place succeeded in pacifying the disorderly crowd. . . .

Astrakhan, September 25. As a result of the reduction of the bread ration, a large crowd went to the opposite bank of the Volga where the gubernia food committee is located, and demanded an explanation from the chairman of the committee. They then broke into the commissariat, fell upon Sklabinsky, the gubernia commissar, and threw him into the street. Sklabinsky was wounded. With the arrival of the Cossacks and militia the crowd was quieted and dispersed. . . .

Saratov, October 18. In Petrovsk, prisoners in jails and detention houses were released by the crowds.

Samara, October 26. In Bugulma, of Samara Gubernia, the wine storehouse, apothecary shops, and stores were demolished. The uezd commissar appealed to Samara and Simbirsk for help.

Ekaterinburg, October 21. In the village of Korabelsky, on account of the dissatisfaction with the grain monopoly, a crowd of peasants wrought havoc in the premises of the volost food committee and seized a member of the food administration. . . .

Omsk, October 19. A military detachment has arrived from Petropavlovsk to put down the riot in the city. Before the arrival of the troops several shops and private homes were destroyed. Dimitriev, the chairman of the city food administration, was killed. . . .

Tashkent, September 27. In connection with the aggravation of the provisions question, a number of soldiers decided to arrest the food manager . . . and his two assistants. It was decided to transfer the business of provisions into the hands of the workers and soldiers and not to permit the shipment of manufactured goods to Bokhara. . . .

— Reading No. 25 —

AN OFFICIAL REPORT ON THE FOOD SHORTAGE [25]

On October 29, S. N. Prokopovich, Minister of Supplies, made the following report on the food situation.

✓   ✓   ✓

. . . I have the following telegram from General Cheremisov: "The food situation at the front is catastrophic. Horses are perishing for lack of forage. Bakeries stop working because there is no flour. The last reserves of hardtack are now being consumed. . . . An epidemic of starvation will break out with all its consequences. Every hour of delay . . . threatens to ruin the army." Such is the situation in spite of the increased purchase of supplies. The reason for it is that between the base of supplies and the army there lies a vast area submerged by anarchy which defeats every regulated effort to supply the army and the population. . . .

I come now to Petrograd. Bread supplies in the capital on October 27 consisted of 152 carloads, with an average daily arrival of twenty to twenty-two cars and a daily consumption of forty cars. . . . We are thus provided

[25] From *Riech,* No. 244, Oct. 30, 1927, as quoted in Bunyan and Fisher, *op. cit.,* pp. 49-50. Reprinted with the permission of the author and of the publishers, Stanford University Press. Copyright 1934 by the Board of Trustees of Leland Stanford Junior University.

for the next seven or eight days, and the rations will continue as before, three-fourths of a pound per day. . . .
In Petrograd we have to face the very disturbing fact that the bread already purchased is not being delivered. . . .
Out of the 400,000 puds shipped to Petrograd by way of the Mariinsky Canal . . . 200,000 puds were either detained or stolen on the way. . . . Here is a telegram from Cherepovets: "Shipments of bread are being plundered by peasants of Novgorod and Olonets gubernias. . . . Soldiers escorting cannot stop. Please take immediate measures to save [the bread]." A telegram from Rybinsk: "This is second time that barge has been stopped . . . by armed peasants who plundered some 120,000 puds of flour. The soldiers who were sent after them refused to bring it back. . . ."

Ordinarily the peasants are forced to sell their grain by economic needs. No such need exists at present, and special measures have to be taken to get the grain. . . . They refuse to give bread not only for the cities but for the army as well. . . .

The minister then read telegrams from Saratov, Samara, and Voronezh. They state that plundering of food trains is very common. . . . Railway employees are compelled, under threat of lynching, to give up freight cars. In Saratov . . . the number of starving people and of speculators is growing larger every day, becoming more and more menacing. The local committee and the Soviet of Workers' and Soldiers' Deputies are helpless to cope with the situation. . . . Local committees [of supply] and railroad employees are especially endangered. The violence of the mob is often directed against them, and they are wholly helpless to offer resistance.

— Reading No. 26 —

AN APPEAL FROM LENIN TO THE MASSES[26]

Lenin continued to pour forth arguments and appeals to the populace to turn away from the Provisional Government and come out for an insurrection. This example of his efforts was written between October 14 and 20, 1917.

✓　　　　✓　　　　✓

TO THE WORKERS, PEASANTS, AND SOLDIERS!

Comrades! The party of the "Socialist-Revolutionaries," to which Kerensky belongs, appeals to you . . . to "be patient."

"One must be patient," the paper writes in urging that power be left in the hands of Kerensky's government, in urging that power should not pass to the Soviets of Workers' and Soldiers' Deputies. Let Kerensky rely on the landowners, capitalists, and kulaks, let the Soviets that have carried through the revolution and vanquished the Kornilovist generals "be patient," we are told. Let them "be patient" until the speedy convocation of the Constituent Assembly.

Comrades! Look around, see what is happening in the village, what is happening in the army, and you will realize that the peasants and the soldiers cannot stand it any longer. Over the whole of Russia, like a broad river, sweeps *an uprising of the peasants,* from whom the land has hitherto been withheld by fraud. The peasants cannot stand it any longer. Kerensky sends *troops* to suppress the peasants and to defend the landowners. Kerensky has

[26] From V. I. Lenin, *Collected Works,* Vol. XXI, Book II (New York, 1932), pp. 59-60. Quoted by permission of International Publishers.

again come to an agreement with the Kornilovist generals and officers who stand for the landowners. . . .

As to what is going on in the army at the front, the officer Dubasov, a nonpartisan, has declared before all of Russia: "The soldiers will not fight any longer." The soldiers are tired out, the soldiers are barefooted, the soldiers are starving, the soldiers do not want to fight for the interests of the capitalists, they do not wish to *"be patient,"* to be treated only to beautiful words about peace, while for months the *peace proposal,* the proposal for a just peace without annexations, to be offered to *all* the belligerent peoples, has been delayed (as is being done by Kerensky). . . .

Go, then, to the barracks, go to the Cossack units, go to the toilers and explain the *truth* to the people:

If power is in the hands of the Soviets, then not later than November 7 . . . *a just peace will be offered* to all the belligerent peoples. There will be in Russia *a workers' and peasants' government;* it will *immediately,* without losing a single day, *offer a just peace to all the belligerent peoples.* Then the people will learn who wishes the unjust war. Then the people will decide in the Constituent Assembly.

If power is in the hands of the Soviets, the *landowners' lands* will immediately be declared the *property and heritage of the whole people.*

This is what Kerensky and his government fight against, basing themselves on the village exploiters, capitalists and landowners! This is what you are called to "be patient" for; these are the interests involved!

Are you willing to "be patient" in order that Kerensky may quell with armed force the peasants who have risen for the land? Are you willing to "be patient" in order that the war may be dragged out longer, the *offer of peace* postponed, the tearing up of the secret treaties of the former Tsar with the Russian and Anglo-French capitalists postponed?

Comrades, remember that Kerensky has already once deceived the people when he promised to convoke the Constituent Assembly! On July 21 he solemnly promised to convoke it not later than September 30, and he has *deceived the people.* Comrades! Whoever believes in the

Kerensky government is a traitor to his brothers, the peasants and soldiers!

No, *not for one more day* are the people willing to suffer postponement, *Not for a single day longer* can we suffer the peasants to be quelled by armed force, thousands upon thousands to perish in the war, when *a just peace can and must be offered at once.*

Down with the government of Kerensky, who is conniving with the Kornilovist landowner-generals to suppress the peasants, to fire on the peasants, to drag out the war!

All power to the Soviet of Workers' and Soldiers' Deputies!

— Reading No. 27 —

AN APPEAL TO THE PETROGRAD GARRISON FROM THE MILITARY REVOLUTIONARY COMMITTEE [27]

The Military Revolutionary Committee set up by the Petrograd Soviet to defend the city against Germans and reactionaries, clashed with the military staff of the Petrograd district. The Committee thereupon appealed to the

[27] From N. Podvoisky, "Voennaia Organizatsiia Ts. K. R.S-D. R. P. (Bol'shevikov) i Voenno-revoliutsionnyi Komitet 1917 g.," *Krasnaia Letopis',* No. 8, 1923, p. 17, as quoted in James Bunyan and H. H. Fisher, *The Bolshevik Revolution, 1917-1918; Documents and Materials* (Stanford, 1918), pp. 81-82. Reprinted with the permission of the author and of the publishers, Stanford University Press. Copyright 1934 by the Board of Trustees of Leland Stanford Junior University.

Petrograd garrison for full support, claiming that the staff was counter-revolutionary.

✓ ✓ ✓

At its meeting on November 3 the revolutionary garrison of Petrograd gathered around the Military Revolutionary Committee of the Petrograd Soviet of Workers' and Soldiers' Deputies as its directive organ.

In spite of this, the staff of the Petrograd Military District refused, during the night preceding November 4, to acknowledge the Military Revolutionary Committee. . . . By this act the staff has broken off relations with the revolutionary garrison as well as with the Petrograd Soviet. Having broken off relations with the organized garrison of the capital, the staff thereby becomes the tool of counter-revolutionary forces.

The Military Revolutionary Committee is thus released from all responsibility for the acts of the staff of the Petrograd Military District.

Soldiers of Petrograd! It is for you, under the direction of the Military Revolutionary Committee, to defend the revolutionary order against counter-revolution. Orders not signed by this committee are void. Every soldier should be on guard and maintain strict discipline. The revolution is in danger! Long live the revolutionary garrison!

— Reading No. 28 —

AN INCENDIARY SPEECH BY TROTSKY ON THE EVE OF THE UPRISING[28]

On November 4, the Day of the Petersburg Soviet, Trotsky, Chairman of the Soviet, spoke to an immense crowd in Petrograd. With fire and brilliance he aroused his audience to ecstatic fervor for the coming revolution. The account is taken from the memoirs of N. N. Sukhanov, a socialist member of the Soviet, who disapproved of the coming insurrection.

↗   ↗   ↗

Trotsky immediately began to inflame the atmosphere—with his skill and brilliance. I remember, he at length and with extraordinary force sketched the picture, difficult in its simplicity, of hardship in the trenches. Before me flashed thoughts of the inevitable incompatibility of the parts in this oratorical whole. But Trotsky knew what he was doing. The essential thing was the frame of mind. The political conclusions had been known for a long time. You could make a mess of them—provided only you did it with sufficient striking effect.

Trotsky did it . . . with sufficient effect. The Soviet power was not only called on to abolish the hardship of the trenches. It would give land and would heal the internal ruination. Once more the remedies against starvation were repeated: a soldier, a sailor, and a working woman, who would requisition bread from the wealthy and send it free to the city and to the front. . . . But Trotsky went even further on the decisive "Day of the Petersburg Soviet."

"The Soviet Power will hand over everything that there is in the country to the poor and to the men in the

[28] From N. N. Sukhanov, *Zapiski o Revoliutsii* (Berlin, 1922-1923), VII, 90-92, translated by J. S. Curtiss.

trenches. You, bourgeois, have two coats—give one to the soldier, who is cold in the trenches. You have warm boots? Stay at home. Your boots are needed by the worker. . . ."

These were very fine and righteous thoughts. They could not help arousing the enthusiasm of the crowd, which had been trained by the Tsarist whip. . . .

Around me was a spirit close to ecstasy. It seemed that the crowd would, at once, without any urging or leadership, sing some sort of religious hymn. . . . Trotsky formulated some sort of short general resolution, or proclaimed some sort of general formula, like "we will stand for the cause of the workers and peasants to our last drop of blood."

Who is in favor? The crowd of thousands, as one man, raised their hands. I saw the raised hands and the burning eyes of men, women, youngsters, workers, soldiers, muzhiks, and—of typically lower middle-class persons. Were they in a soulful passion? Did they see, through the raised curtain, a corner of some sort of "holy land" toward which they were striving? Or were they imbued with a consciousness of the *political moment,* under the influence of the political agitation of the socialist? Do not ask! Accept it as it was. . . .

Trotsky continued to speak. The uncounted throng continued to hold their hands high. Trotsky rang forth the words:

"Let this your voting be your oath—with all your strength, at any cost to support the Soviet, which is taking upon itself the great burden of carrying to a conclusion the victory of the revolution and to give land, bread, and peace!"

The countless crowd held high their hands. They agreed. They pledged themselves. . . . Again, just take it as it was: I with an unusually heavy feeling looked on this truly magnificent picture.

Trotsky finished. Some other person came out on the platform. But there was no reason to wait and watch any longer.

In all Petrograd approximately the same thing was happening. Everywhere there were the final inspections and the final oaths. Thousands, tens of thousands, hundreds of thousands of people. . . . This, in reality, was already an insurrection. The affair had already begun.

— Reading No. 29 —

THE FALL OF THE
WINTER PALACE [29]

The commanders of the Red forces, in spite of their overwhelming numbers, violated all rules of strategy by delaying for many hours to attack the Winter Palace, the last stronghold of the Provisional Government. When the attack did come, it found the defenses woefully weak. The conquest of the palace was accomplished largely by infiltration rather than by outright fighting. The utter helplessness of the Provisional Government was clearly shown in this episode.

1   1   1

. . . The old Provisional Government was still languishing in a quiet, half-dark room of the Winter Palace. It had not decided to die. On the contrary, it hoped for aid and for the protection of their lives and positions. But nevertheless it languished in misery.

The Cossacks went away out of the palace. The defenders were declining in numbers. We were informed by telephone that the town councillors and others, to the number of about 300 persons, were coming from the city Duma. The cadets were warned not to shoot at them. . . .

Palchinsky reported: a crowd had tried to break in several times, but after shots from the cadets they had retired. They were said to be shooting in the air. But the crackle of rifles and roar of cannon became more and more frequent. Suddenly there was commotion and shots in the palace itself; from thirty to forty armed men had broken in, but they had been disarmed and taken prisoner.

"They are great cowards," Palchinsky reports, and assures us that the palace will hold out until morning.

[29] From N. N. Sukhanov, *Zapiski o Revoliutsii* (Berlin, 1923), VII, 209-215, translated by J. S. Curtiss.

Again commotion, shouts, stamping, and—one after another, two explosions. The ministers jumped from their seats. Grenades! Several sailors had broken into the palace and had thrown two grenades from a little gallery. . . . They . . . had lightly wounded two cadets. Dr. Shishkin gave them first aid. The sailors were taken prisoner. But how could they get in? First forty men had forced their way in, now a number of sailors had entered secretly. Evidently, Palchinsky and his garrison were not very effective.

It was reported that the woman's shock battalion had gone home. They wished to and they went, like the Cossacks. Evidently the besieging army let through hostile detachments, as a sieve does water. As yet there was no siege.

But the firing began to take on the character of a real battle. It was unbelievable that they were only firing in the air and that there were no casualties. Bloodshed on some scale or other was undoubtedly occurring. Why, for what reason? Because the Military Revolutionary Committee had not thought to arrest the Provisional Government earlier and had even released those taken prisoner. And also so the ministers who had fled from their posts could console themselves with the thought that they had not fled.

It was reported that the cadets of such-and-such a school had gone. They had just walked away. The "Government" had not restrained them, but it was sending bulletins to the city by telephone: We are beating them off, we are not giving up, an attack was repelled at such-and-such an hour, we are expecting reenforcements. . . . This is the sort of leaders we had!

Once more commotion in the corridors. About 100 "Bolsheviks" had broken in. The defenders had taken them for the deputation from the Duma. The enemy troop permitted itself to be disarmed without trouble. . . . It was reported: the cadets of such-and-such a school have left. One cannot but note: the opposing sides are fanatically inspired and fight like lions. . . .

Again commotion below. It grows—nearer and nearer It is already in the . . . corridor, and rolls on, growing, to the very doors. Evidently, they have "stormed" the palace and "taken" it. A cadet dashes in to the ministers and, drawing himself up, reports: "We are ready to defend ourselves to the last man. What does the Provisional Government order?"

"You must not, it is useless. We'll surrender. No more blood must be shed. Surely the palace is already taken?"

"It's taken. All have surrendered. Only this room is defended."

"Say that we do not want bloodshed and will surrender. We give up to superior force. Go, go, hurry. We do not want bloodshed!" . . .

The cadet through the door reported the decision of the ministers to the victorious insurgent troops, which shouted unrestrainedly, but did not advance a step against the will of these determined cadets. . . .

"Let's sit at the table," said one of the ministers, and they sat down in order to look like busy men of state.

The doors burst open. The room at once was filled with armed men with Antonov himself at their head. . . . "I declare to you, members of the Provisional Government, that you are under arrest," shouted Antonov. "I am a member of the Military Revolutionary Committee."

"The members of the Provisional Government submit to violence and surrender, in order to avoid bloodshed," said Konovalov.

"Bloodshed! But how much blood you yourselves have shed!" burst forth an exclamation, sympathetically echoed by the crowd. "How many of our men have fallen!" . . .

The frame of mind of the crowd that had broken in, armed from head to foot, was very excited, vengeful, hostile, unstable. Antonov was pacifying the soldiers and sailors that were especially beside themselves, but he did not have enough authority. They began to draw up a protocol. . . . The frame of mind now became excited, now calmed down. The information that Kerensky was not there had a strong effect. Shouts were uttered that they should bayonet all the others, so they could not flee after Kerensky.

After a rather long procedure of questioning, listing, rollcalls, they set out in a prisoners' column . . . to the Fortress of Peter and Paul. In darkness, at 3 A.M., through a thick, excited crowd the column moved along. . . . More than once the lives of the former ministers hung on a hair. But it went off without a lynching.

After eight months of the revolution the Peter and Paul was receiving the third kind of prisoners within its walls: first the Tsarist functionaries, then the Bolsheviks, now the friends of Kerensky, the "chosen" of the Menshevik-S. R. democracy. What more would these unmoving walls still see?

— Reading No. 30 —

ORDER TO DUKHONIN TO OPEN ARMISTICE NEGOTIATIONS [30]

At army headquarters at the front, General N. N. Dukhonin, the Commander-in-Chief, refused to accept the commands of the new government. On November 21, the Soviet leaders wired him instructions to begin armistice negotiations at once with the Germans. He, however, was unwilling to do this.

✦   ✦   ✦

Citizen Supreme Commander-in-Chief!

In accordance with instructions from the All-Russian Congress of Soviets of Workers' and Soldiers' Deputies, the Soviet of People's Commissars has assumed the authority, as well as the obligation of proposing to all warring nations and their governments an immediate truce on all fronts and an immediate opening of negotiations with the object of peace on democratic principles.

[30] From S. A. Piontkovskii, *Khrestomatiia po Istorii Okt'iabrskoi Revoliutsii*, p. 265, as quoted in Bunyan and Fisher, *op. cit.*, p. 233. Reprinted with the permission of the author and of the publishers, Stanford University Press. Copyright 1934 by the Board of Trustees of Leland Stanford Junior University.

At present, with the Soviet power firmly established at all the most important points throughout the country, the Soviet of People's Commissars finds it necessary to make at once formal proposals for an armistice to all the warring nations, allied and enemy. A note to this effect has been dispatched by the People's Commissariat of Foreign Affairs to all the plenipotentiary envoys of the Allied countries in Petrograd.

Immediately after the receipt of this communication you, citizen Supreme Commander-in-Chief, are ordered by the Soviet of People's Commissars, in compliance with the resolution of the All-Russian Congress of Soviets of Workers' and Soldiers' Deputies, to address yourself to the military authorities of the enemy armies with the proposal of an immediate cessation of hostilities for the purpose of starting peace negotiations. In entrusting you with the conduct of these preliminary pourparlers, the Soviet of People's Commissars orders you: *First,* to keep the Soviet constantly informed by direct wire of the progress of your pourparlers with the representatives of the enemy armies, and *secondly,* to sign a truce only after obtaining the consent of the Soviet of People's Commissars.

> **V.** Ulianov (Lenin), President of the Soviet
> of People's Commissars
> **L.** Trotsky, Commissar of Foreign Affairs
> Krylenko, Commissar of War

— Reading No. 31 —

MEETING OF THE PETROGRAD SOVIET[31]

[31] From *Izvestiia,* No. 207, Nov. 8, 1917, as quoted in Frank Alfred Golder, *Documents of Russian History* (New York, 1927), pp. 617-619. Quoted by permission of Appleton-Century-Crofts, Inc.

On the afternoon of November 7 the Petrograd Soviet met in triumph. Trotsky, somewhat prematurely, proclaimed complete victory over the Provisional Government. He was followed on the platform by Lenin, who announced his program of future action.

✓   ✓   ✓

The meeting opened at 2:35 P.M. with Trotsky in the chair. He said: "In the name of the Military Revolutionary Committee, I announce the Provisional Government no longer exists. (Applause.) Some of the Ministers are already under arrest. (Bravo.) Others soon will be. (Applause.) The revolutionary garrison, under the control of the Military Revolutionary Committee, has dismissed the Assembly of the Pre-Parliament. (Loud applause. "Long live the Military Revolutionary Committee."). . . . The railway stations, post and telegraph offices, the Petrograd Telegraph Agency, and State Bank are occupied. . . ."

Trotsky continued by saying: "In our midst is Vladimir Ilich Lenin, who, by force of circumstances, had not been able to be with us all this time. . . . Hail the return of Lenin!" The audience gave him a noisy ovation. . . . [Lenin spoke as follows:]

Comrades, the workmen's and peasants' revolution, the need of which the Bolsheviks have emphasized many times, has come to pass.

What is the significance of this revolution? Its significance is, in the first place, that we shall have a soviet government, without the participation of bourgeoisie of any kind. The oppressed masses will of themselves form a government. The old state machinery will be smashed into bits and in its place will be created a new machinery of government by the soviet organizations. From now on there is a new page in the history of Russia, and the present, third Russian revolution shall in the final result lead to the victory of Socialism.

One of our immediate tasks is to put an end to the war at once. But in order to end the war, which is closely bound up with the present capitalistic system, it is necessary to overthrow capitalism itself. In this work we shall have the aid of the world labor movement, which has already begun to develop in Italy, England, and Germany.

A just and immediate offer of peace by us to the international democracy will find everywhere a warm response among the international proletariat masses. In order to secure the confidence of the proletariat, it is necessary to publish at once all the secret treaties.

In the interior of Russia a very large part of the peasantry has said: Enough playing with the capitalists; we will go with the workers. We shall secure the confidence of the peasants by one decree, which will wipe out the private property of the landowners. The peasants will understand that their only salvation is in union with the workers.

We will establish a real labor control on production.

We have now learned to work together in a friendly manner, as is evident from this revolution. We have the force of mass organization, which has conquered all and which will lead the proletariat to world revolution.

We shall now occupy ourselves in Russia in building up a proletarian socialist state.

Long live the world-wide socialistic revolution!

— Reading No. 32 —

JOHN REED'S ACCOUNT OF THE OPENING OF THE SECOND CONGRESS OF SOVIETS [32]

John Reed, the noted American Socialist, was present as a newspaper correspondent at the opening of the Congress of Soviets. He vividly portrays the bitterness with which the moderate socialists repudiated the Bolshevik in-

[32] From John Reed, *Ten Days That Shook the World* (London, 1934), pp. 73-78. Quoted by permission of International Publishers.

surrection, and the doubts of the proletarians as one speaker after another accused them of ruining the cause of the Revolution. Finally, a message of encouragement from the army at the front heartened the insurgent delegates by convincing them that the former speakers had not spoken for the whole country and that the new revolution had much mass support.

$\checkmark$ $\checkmark$ $\checkmark$

So we came into the great meeting-hall, pushing through the clamorous mob at the door. In the rows of seats, under the white chandeliers, packed immovably in the aisles and on the sides, perched on every window-sill, and even on the edge of the platform, the representatives of the workers and soldiers of all Russia waited in anxious silence or wild exultation for the ringing of the chairman's bell. There was no heat in the hall but the stifling heat of unwashed human bodies. A foul blue cloud of cigarette smoke rose from the mass and hung in the thick air. Occasionally someone in authority mounted the tribune and asked the comrades not to smoke; then everybody, smokers and all, took up the cry, "Don't smoke, comrades!" and went on smoking. Petrovsky, Anarchist delegate from the Obukhov factory, made a seat for me beside him. Unshaven and filthy, he was reeling from three nights' sleepless work on the Military Revolutionary Committee. . . .

But suddenly a new sound made itself heard, deeper than the tumult of the crowd, persistent, disquieting—the dull shock of guns. People looked anxiously toward the clouded windows, and a sort of fever came over them. Martov, demanding the floor, croaked hoarsely, "The civil war is beginning, comrades! The first question must be a peaceful settlement of the crisis. On principle and from a political standpoint we must urgently discuss a means of averting civil war. Our brothers are being shot down in the streets! At this very moment, when before the opening of the Congress of Soviets the question of Power is being settled by means of a military plot organised by one of the revolutionary parties—" for a moment he could not make himself heard above the noise, "All of the revolutionary parties must face the fact! The first vopros (question) before the Congress is the question of Power, and this question is already being settled by force of arms in the streets! . . . We must create a power which will be recognised by the whole democracy. If the Congress wishes to be the voice of the revolutionary democracy it must not sit with folded hands before the developing civil war, the result of which may be a dangerous outburst of counter-revolution. . . . The possibility of a peaceful outcome lies in the formation of a united democratic authority. . . . We must elect a delegation to negotiate with the other Socialist parties and organisations. . . ."

Always the methodical muffled boom of cannon through the windows, and the delegates, screaming at each other. . . . So, with the crash of artillery, in the dark, with hatred, and fear, and reckless daring, new Russia was being born. . . .

On behalf of the Mensheviki, Khintchuk then announced that the only possibility of a peaceful solution was to begin negotiations at once with the Provisional Government for the formation of a new Cabinet, which would find support in all strata of society. He could not proceed for several minutes. Raising his voice to a shout he read the Menshevik declarations:

"Because the Bolsheviki have made a military conspiracy with the aid of the Petrograd Soviet, without consulting the other factions and parties, we find it impossible to remain in the Congress, and therefore withdraw, inviting the other groups to follow us and to meet for discussion of the situation!"

"Deserter!" At intervals in the almost continuous disturbance Hendelman, for the Socialist Revolutionaries, could be heard protesting against the bombardment of the Winter Palace. . . . "We are opposed to this kind of anarchy. . . ."

Scarcely had he stepped down when a young, lean-faced soldier, with flashing eyes, leaped to the platform, and dramatically raised his hand:

"Comrades!" he cried, and there was a hush. "My *familia* (name) is Peterson—I speak for the Second Lettish Rifles. You have heard the statements of two representatives of the Army committees; these statements would have some value *if their authors had been representatives of the Army—*" Wild applause. *"But they do not represent the soldiers!"* Shaking his fist. "The Twelfth Army has been insisting for a long time upon the re-election of the Great Soviet and the Army Committee, but just as your own *Tsay-ee-kah* [Central Executive Committee], our Committee refused to call a meeting of the masses until the end of September, so that the reactionaries could elect their own false delegates to this Congress. I tell you now, the Lettish soldiers have many times said, 'No more resolutions! No more talk! We want deeds—the Power must be in our hands!' Let these impostor delegates leave the Congress! The Army is not with them!"

The hall rocked with cheering. In the first moments of the session, stunned by the rapidity of events, startled by the sound of cannon, the delegates had hesitated. For an hour hammer-blow after hammer-blow had fallen from that tribune, welding them together but beating them down. Did they then stand alone? Was Russia rising against them? Was it true that the Army was marching on Petrograd? Then this clear-eyed young soldier had spoken, and in a flash they knew it for the truth. . . . *This* was the voice of the soldiers—the stirring millions of workers and peasants were men like them, and their thoughts and feelings were the same. . . .

— Reading No. 33 —

THE PROCLAMATION OF THE SOVIET REGIME[33]

[33] From *Vtoroi Vserossiiskii S"ezd Sovetov R. i S. D.* (Moscow, Leningrad, 1928), as quoted in Bunyan and Fisher, *op. cit.*, pp. 121-122. Reprinted with the permission of the author and of the publishers, Stanford University Press. Copyright 1934 by the Board of Trustees of Leland Stanford Junior University.

As soon as the Provisional Government had fallen, the Second Congress of Soviets issued a proclamation to the people setting forth its program and urging them to be zealous in supporting it.

✸   ✸   ✸

To All Workers, Soldiers, and Peasants:

The Second All-Russian Congress of Soviets of Workers' and Soldiers' Deputies has opened. It represents the great majority of the Soviets, including a number of deputies of peasant Soviets. The prerogatives of the Central Executive Committee of the compromisers are ended.

Supported by an overwhelming majority of the workers, soldiers, and peasants, and basing itself on the victorious insurrection of the workers and the garrison of Petrograd, the Congress hereby resolves to take governmental power into its hands.

The Provisional Government is deposed and most of its members are under arrest.

The Soviet authority will at once propose a democratic peace to all nations and an immediate armistice on all fronts. It will safeguard the transfer without compensation of all land—landlord, appanage, and monastery—to the peasant committees; it will defend the soldiers' rights, introducing complete democratization of the army, it will establish workers' control over industry, it will insure the convocation of the Constituent Assembly on the date set, it will supply the cities with bread and the villages with articles of first necessity, and it will secure to all nationalities inhabiting Russia the right of self-determination.

The Congress resolves that all local authority shall be transferred to the Soviets of Workers', Soldiers', and Peasants' Deputies, which are charged with the task of enforcing revolutionary order.

The Congress calls upon the soldiers in the trenches to be watchful and steadfast. The Congress of Soviets is confident that the revolutionary army will know how to defend the revolution against all imperialistic attempts until the new government has concluded a democratic peace which it is proposing directly to all nations.

The new government will take every measure to provide the revolutionary army with all necessities, by means of a

determined policy of requisition from and taxation of
the propertied classes. Care will be taken to improve the
position of the soldiers' families.

The Kornilovists—Kerensky, Kaledin, and others—are
endeavoring to lead troops against Petrograd. Several
regiments, deceived by Kerensky, have already joined
the insurgents.

Soldiers! Resist Kerensky, who is a Kornilovist! Be on
guard!

Railwaymen! Stop all echelons sent by Kerensky against
Petrograd!

Soldiers, Workers, Employees! The fate of the Revolution and democratic peace is in your hands!

Long live the Revolution!

THE ALL-RUSSIAN CONGRESS OF SOVIETS
OF WORKERS' AND SOLDIERS' DEPUTIES
DELEGATES FROM THE PEASANTS' SOVIETS

— Reading No. 34 —

LENIN'S REPORT ON PEACE[34]

*As soon as the Soviet regime had been established,
Lenin hastened to take up the question of peace. On
November 8, 1917, he spoke on the subject and proposed
a Decree on Peace, which was promptly adopted.*

↗   ↗   ↗

The question of peace is a burning and painful question
of the day. Much has been said and written on the subject, and all of you, no doubt, have discussed it quite a

[34] From *Pravda*, No. 171, Nov. 10, 1917, as quoted in *Lenin,
Stalin, 1917. Selected Writings and Speeches* (Moscow,
1938), pp. 618-620.

lot. Permit me, therefore, to read a declaration which the government you elect should publish.

Decree on Peace

The workers' and peasants' government created by the revolution of November 6-7 . . . calls upon all the belligerent nations and their governments to start immediate negotiations for a just, democratic peace.

By a just or democratic peace, for which the overwhelming majority of the working and toiling classes of all the belligerent countries, exhausted, tormented, and racked by the war, are craving—a peace that has been most definitely and insistently demanded by the Russian workers and peasants ever since the overthrow of the tsarist monarchy—the government means an immediate peace without annexations (*i.e.,* the seizure of foreign lands, or the forcible incorporation of foreign nations) and without indemnities.

The government of Russia calls upon all the belligerent nations to conclude such a peace immediately, and expresses its readiness to take the most resolute measures without the least delay, pending the final ratification of the terms of this peace by authoritative assemblies of the people's representatives of all countries and all nations. . . .

The government considers it the greatest of crimes against humanity to continue this war for the purpose of dividing up among the strong and rich nations the feeble nationalities they have conquered, and solemnly announces its determination immediately to sign terms of peace to stop this war on the conditions indicated, which are equally just for all nationalities without exception. . . .

The government abolishes secret diplomacy, and, for its part, announces its firm intention to conduct all negotiations quite openly under the eyes of the whole people. It will immediately proceed to the full publication of the secret treaties. . . . The government proclaims the absolute and immediate annulment of everything contained in these secret treaties that is aimed, as is mostly the case, for securing advantages and privileges for the Russian landlords and capitalists and at the retention, or extension, of the annexations made by the Great-Russians.

Appealing to the governments and peoples of all countries immediately to begin open negotiations for peace, the government, for its part, announces its readiness to conduct these negotiations both in writing, by telegraph, and by negotiations between representatives of the various countries, or at a conference of such representatives. In order to facilitate such negotiations, the government is appointing its authoritative representative to neutral countries.

The government proposes an immediate armistice to the governments and peoples of all the belligerent countries, and, for its part, considers it desirable that this armistice should be concluded for a period of not less than three months, *i.e.*, a period long enough to permit the completion of negotiations for peace . . . and the summoning of authoritative assemblies of the representatives of the peoples of all countries for the final ratification of the terms of peace. . . .

— Reading No. 35 —

LENIN'S REPORT ON THE LAND[35]

Immediately after the Peace Decree Lenin made a report on the land problem, accompanied by a decree and a set of Instructions. This also was quickly approved.

↗   ↗   ↗

We consider that the revolution has demonstrated and proved how important it is that the land questions should be stated clearly. The outbreak of armed insurrection, the second, or October, revolution, clearly proves that the land must be handed over to the peasants. The government that

[35] From *Pravda*, No. 171, Nov. 10, 1917, as quoted in *Lenin, Stalin, 1917, op. cit.*, pp. 625-628.

has been overthrown and the compromising parties of the Mensheviks and Socialist-Revolutionaries committed a crime when they kept postponing the settlement of the land question on various pretexts and thereby brought the country to a state of ruin and confronted it with a peasant revolt. . . . If the government had acted wisely, and if their measures had met the needs of the poor peasants, would there have been unrest among the peasant masses? But all the measures of the government . . . went counter to the interests of the peasants and compelled them to revolt.

. . . The first duty of the government of the workers' and peasants' revolution must be to settle the land question, which can pacify and satisfy the vast mass of poor peasants. I shall read you the points of a decree your Soviet government must promulgate. In one of the points of this decree are embodied the Instructions to the Land Committees which have been compiled from 242 Instructions from local Soviets of Peasants' Deputies.

Decree on the Land

1. Landed proprietorship is abolished forthwith without compensation.

2. The landed estates, as also all crown, monasterial and church lands, with all their livestock, implements, farm buildings, and everything pertaining thereto, shall be placed at the disposal of the rural Land Committees and the district Soviets of Peasants' Deputies pending the convocation of the Constituent Assembly.

3. All damage to confiscated property, which henceforth belongs to the whole people, is proclaimed a felony punishable by the revolutionary courts. . . .

4. The following peasant Instructions . . . shall everywhere serve as a guide in carrying through the great land reforms until a final decision is taken on the latter by the Constituent Assembly.

5. The land of ordinary peasants and ordinary Cossacks shall not be confiscated.

— Reading No. 36 —

DECREE ON THE TRANSFERRING OF ECONOMIC POWER TO THE TOILERS [36]

About ten days after the founding of the Soviet regime, the Council of People's Commissars issued a decree on the transfer of economic power to the laboring people. This decree, which was addressed to the masses, was couched in general terms rather than in the form of a law. It assured the working people that the victory of the revolution was certain and that they should actively support the Soviets. Above all, they should be vigilant to crush economic sabotage and to protect the nation's wealth.

✓   ✓   ✓

Comrades—Workers, Soldiers, Peasants, All Toilers!

The workers' and peasants' revolution has won a decisive victory in Petrograd. . . . The revolution has triumphed in Moscow. . . . An overwhelming majority of soldiers in the trenches and peasants in the villages are supporting the new government in its peace decree and its decree to hand over immediately the land to peasants. The victory of the workers' and peasants' revolution is assured; the majority of the people are for it.

It is easy to understand why the landowners, the capitalists, and the higher state officials who are closely bound up with the bourgeoisie—in one word, all the rich and those who hold out their hands to the rich—should

[36] From *Sobranie Uzakonenii i Rasporiazhenii Rabochego i Krestianskago Pravitel'stva*, 1917, as quoted in Bunyan and Fisher, *op. cit.*, pp. 277-279. Reprinted with the permission of the author and of the publishers, Stanford University Press. Copyright 1934 by the Board of Trustees of Leland Stanford Junior University.

assume a hostile attitude toward the new revolution . . . and should threaten to close the banks and to stop or to sabotage, directly or indirectly, the work of various institutions.

Every class-conscious worker knows full well that this opposition is inevitable, that the higher officials were selected to oppress the people, and that they are not going to give up their place without a struggle. The laboring classes will not allow themselves to be frightened, even for a minute, by the threats and strikes of these partisans of the bourgeoisie. The majority of the people are with us. With us are the majority of the toilers, and the oppressed of the world. Right is on our side. Our victory is certain. The opposition of the capitalists and higher officials will be broken. We will not deprive a single person of his property otherwise than by a special government law concerning the nationalization of banks and trusts. This law is now in preparation. Not a single laborer and toiler will lose one kopeck; on the contrary, he will be helped. The government will impose no new taxes now and will aim at an open and strict accounting and control over the taxes heretofore levied.

In the name of these just demands the great majority of the people has rallied around the Provisional Workers' and Peasants' Government.

Comrade Toilers! Remember that you yourself are now running the government. Unless you get together and take all affairs of the government into your own hands, no one will do it for you. Your Soviets are from now on all-powerful and all-decisive organs of government. Rally around your Soviets. Strengthen them. Take matters into your own hands and don't wait for anyone. Insist on the strictest revolutionary order. Crush mercilessly all anarchistic disturbances by drunkards, rowdies, counter-revolutionary cadets, Kornilovists, and their like.

Organize strict control over production and accountability for the products. Bring before the revolutionary tribunal everyone who dares to harm the cause of the people by sabotaging (spoiling, hindering, destroying) in industry, concealing grain and produce, interfering with transportation of grain, tearing up rail, post, and telegraph lines, or in other ways opposing the great cause of peace, of transferring the land to the peasants, and of assuming workers' control over production and distribution.

Comrade workers, soldiers, peasants, and all toilers! Take all local power into your own hands. Take and guard as the apple of your eye the grain, factories, implements, products, and transport—all these are from now on wholly yours; they are public property.

Gradually, with the approval and agreement of the majority of the peasants, guided by their practical experience and that of the workers, we shall move on firmly and resolutely to the victory of socialism, a victory which the advance guard of the workers of the more civilized countries will make secure and which is bound to give the people a lasting peace and freedom from all oppression and exploitation.

V. Ulianov (Lenin)
President of the Soviet of People's
Commissars

— Reading No. 37 —

PASTORAL LETTER OF PATRIARCH TIKHON [37]

The Russian Orthodox church, headed by Patriarch Tikhon, repeatedly spoke out against the Bolsheviks, both before and after the revolution of November 7, 1917. Although the Soviet government made no effort to suppress the Russian church or other religious bodies, its confiscation of church property and other acts produced the Patriarch's Pastoral Letter of February 1, 1918, which was couched in especially uncompromising terms.

✓   ✓   ✓

[37] From A. I. Vvedenskii, *Tserkov' i Gosudarstvo* (Moscow, 1923), pp. 114-116, translated by J. S. Curtiss.

The humble Tikhon, by the grace of God Patriarch of Moscow and All Russia, to all God's beloved: prelates, priests, and all faithful children of the Russian Orthodox church:

. . . That He might deliver us from this present evil world. . . . (*Gal. 1:4*).

The Holy Orthodox Christian Church is passing through a difficult period. The open and concealed enemies of the truth of Christ have started to persecute that truth and are aiming a mortal blow at the cause of Christ, and in place of Christian love they are everywhere sowing seeds of malice, envy, and fratricidal war.

Christ's commandment to love our neighbor is forgotten and trampled under foot. Every day we learn that innocent people, not excluding those confined to their beds, are being frightfully and brutally murdered for the sole offense that they had honestly discharged their duty to the country. . . . These crimes are committed . . . in broad daylight with unprecedented effrontery and outrageous brutality . . . in almost every city of our native land. . . .

These crimes fill the heart with deep sorrow and compel us to denounce these outcasts of the human race . . . in accordance with the command of the Holy Apostle: "Them that sin reprove in the sight of all, that the rest may also be in fear" (*I Tim. 5:20*).

Think what you are doing, you madmen! Cease your bloody attacks. Your acts are not merely cruel, they are the works of Satan, for which you will burn in hell fire in the life hereafter and be cursed by future generations in this life.

By the authority given me by God I forbid you to partake of the Christian Mysteries, I anathematize if you still bear a Christian name and belong, if only by birth, to the Orthodox Church.

And you, faithful children of the Orthodox Christian Church, I beseech you to have nothing in common with these outcasts of the human race: "Put away the wicked man from among yourselves." (*I Cor. 5:12*.)

Violent persecution is being committed against the Orthodox Christian Church; the blessed sacraments which sanctify the birth of man or the union of husband and wife in a Christian family, are openly declared unnecessary and superfluous; holy churches are being destroyed by gunfire (churches of the Moscow Kremlin), or looted and desecrated (the chapel of Our Savior in Petrograd); monasteries most revered by the faithful, such as the Alexandro-Nevskaia and the Pochaevskaia Lavras, have been seized by the godless rulers of darkness under the pretext that they are the people's property. . . .

Is there no limit to this abuse of the Orthodox Church? How is it possible to end the aggressiveness of its raging enemies?

I call on all of you, believing and true sons of the Church: stand in defense of our Holy Mother, now outraged and oppressed. . . . And if it will even be necessary to suffer for the cause of Christ, we call on you, beloved sons of the Church, we call on you together with ourselves to these sufferings in the words of the Holy Apostle: "Who now can deprive you of the love of God? Grief, or bonds, or oppression, or hunger, or nakedness, or calamity, or the sword?" (*Rom. 8:35.*)

And you, brother Archpastors and pastors, without delaying in your spiritual action for one hour, with flaming faith call our sons to defend the rights, now trampled on, of the Orthodox Church, immediately organize religious leagues, call them, not out of need, but from good will, to range themselves in the ranks of the spiritual fighters, who to external force will oppose the strength of their holy inspiration, and we firmly trust that the enemies of the Church of Christ will be broken and scattered by the force of the Cross of Christ, for immutable is the promise of the Divine Crossbearer Himself: "I will build my Church, and the gates of Hell shall not prevail against it." (*Matt. 16:18.*)

— Reading No. 38 —

SEPARATION OF CHURCH AND STATE[38]

Only on February 5, 1918, did the Sovnarkom issue a decree providing for separation of church and state. Although it was much more drastic than the corresponding legislation elsewhere, it was not an effort to wipe out religious observance in toto. While the church buildings were declared national property, the religious organizations were permitted to use them gratis *for holding services.*

1. The church is separated from the state.

2. Within the territory of the Republic the passing of any local laws or regulations interfering with freedom of conscience or granting special rights or privileges to citizens because they belong to a certain faith, is forbidden.

3. Every citizen has a right to adopt any religion or not to adopt any at all. Every legal restriction connected with the profession of certain faiths or with the non-profession of any faith is now abolished.

Note. Official acts shall make no mention of a citizen's faith.

4. State or semi-official public functions are not to be accompanied by religious ceremonies or rituals.

5. Religious performances may be carried on freely in so far as they do not disturb the public order or encroach upon the rights of citizens of the Russian Republic.

[38] From *Sobranie Uzakonenii i Rasporiazhenii*, No. 18, 1918, pp. 272-273, as quoted in Bunyan and Fisher, *op. cit.*, pp. 590-591. Reprinted with the permission of the author and of the publishers, Stanford University Press. Copyright 1934 by the Board of Trustees of Leland Stanford Junior University.

Local authorities have the right to take the necessary measures to preserve order and safeguard the rights of citizens.

6. No one can decline to carry out his civic duties on the ground of his religious views. Exception to this ruling may be made by special decisions of the people's court, provided one civic duty is substituted for another.

7. Religious oaths are abolished. In case of necessity a solemn promise will suffice.

8. All civil acts are performed exclusively by the civil authorities of the department for the registration of marriages and births.

9. The school is separated from the church. The teaching of religion in state and public schools, as well as in private schools where general subjects are taught, is forbidden. Citizens may study or teach religious subjects privately.

10. Church and religious societies are subject to the same laws and regulations as private societies and unions. They do not enjoy any special privileges or subsidies from the state or from local institutions.

11. (Omitted.)

12. Church and religious societies have no right to own property. They do not have the rights of a legal person.

13. All property in Russia now owned by churches and religious organizations is henceforth the property of the people. Buildings and objects that are needed for religious services revert to the free use of religious organizations by special arrangement with the central or local Soviet authorities.

— Reading No. 39 —

LENIN'S REPORT TO THE THIRD CONGRESS OF SOVIETS[39]

On January 24, 1918, Lenin, speaking for the Council of People's Commissars, reported to the Third Congress of Soviets on the results of the first two and one-half months of the Soviet regime. He laid the successes of the period chiefly to the support given by the peasants.

↗   ↗   ↗

Comrades! In the name of the Soviet of People's Commissars I wish to report on two and one-half months of that body's activity. . . .

Two and one-half months is only five days longer than the period during which the Paris Commune of 1871 existed. . . . The workers of Paris . . . were shot by the French Cadets, Mensheviks, the Socialist-Revolutionists of the Right. . . . We find ourselves in more favorable conditions, because the Russian soldiers, workers, and peasants have formed a . . . Soviet Government, . . . which has the support of an overwhelming majority of the masses and is therefore unconquerable.

The betrayers of the revolution, . . . those who doubted the possibility of a Soviet Government, strained their throats in clamoring that, alone, the proletariat could not maintain itself in power. As if we Bolsheviks . . . ever overlooked the fact that only by forming . . . a union of the proletariat and the poor peasants can a government maintain itself in power. . . . This we suc-

[39] From *Tretii Vserossiiskii S"ezd Sovetov Rabochikh, Soldatskikh, i Krest'ianskikh Deputatov* (Petrograd, 1918), pp. 90-92, as quoted in Bunyan and Fisher, *op. cit.*, pp. 391-393. Reprinted with the permission of the author and of the publishers, Stanford University Press. Copyright 1934 by the Board of Trustees of Leland Stanford Junior University.

ceeded in accomplishing immediately after November 7, and we organized a government on the basis of such a union.

. . . When the time came to put socialism into practice the peasants were confronted with two alternatives of political association—either with the bourgeoisie or with the working class—and they soon perceived that the party which more fully expressed the genuine aspirations and interests of the peasantry was the party of the Socialist-Revolutionists of the Left. (*Applause*) We then concluded an alliance with that party. . . . If the Russian peasants wish to bring about the socialization of land in alliance with the workers, who are putting into effect the nationalization of banks and workers' control of industry, they are our true allies, our most faithful and valuable allies. . . .

. . . The experience of civil war has convinced the representatives of the peasants [the Left S. R.'s] that there is no other way to socialism but the dictatorship of the proletariat. . . .

Comrades! Every time I speak on this subject of proletarian government someone . . . shouts "Dictator." Yet [there was a time] . . . when everybody was in favor of the dictatorship of the proletariat. . . . You cannot expect . . . that socialism will be delivered on a silver platter. . . . Not a single question pertaining to the class struggle has ever been settled except by violence. Violence when it is committed by the toiling and exploited masses is the kind of violence of which we approve. (*Shouts of applause.*) . . .

Who ever believed that it was possible to jump at once from capitalism to socialism? . . . Those who understand the nature of class war and sabotage know that this cannot be done. . . . Socialism cannot succeed unless these groups are broken up, unless the bourgeoisie—Russian and European—is crushed. . . .

Of course the socialist idea cannot be attained in one country only. The workers and peasants who support the Soviet Government are only a fragment of that international workers' army which has become divided during this world war. . . . But [the workers of the world] . . . know that Russia is struggling for the common cause, for the cause of the . . . international socialist revolution, . . . and we can see how the socialist revolution is ripen-

ing in every country of the world by hours and not by
days. . . .

— Reading No. 40 —

THE TREATY OF BREST-LITOVSK [40]

*The terms of the Treaty of Brest-Litovsk between
Russia and the Central powers, which was signed on
March 3, 1918, are given below.*

ARTICLE 1. Germany, Austria-Hungary, Bulgaria,
and Turkey on the one hand and Russia on the other declare that the condition of war between them has ceased.
They have decided to live in peace and accord in the
future.

ARTICLE 2. The contracting parties will refrain from
all agitation or propaganda against the governments or all
state and military institutions of the other side. . . .

ARTICLE 3. The territories lying to the west of the
line determined by the contracting powers and which
formerly belonged to Russia will no longer be under her
sovereignty. . . . Russia gives up all interference in the
internal affairs of the said countries. Germany and Austria-Hungary intend to determine the future fate of the
said territories with the consent of their inhabitants.

ARTICLE 4. Germany is ready, as soon as general
peace is established and Russian demobilization will have
completely taken place, to vacate the territories lying east
of the line mentioned in . . . article 3. . . .

[40] From *Papers Relating to the Foreign Relations of the United
States. 1918. Russia* (Washington, D. C., 1931), I, 442-
444.

Russia will do all in her power to have the provinces of eastern Anatolia promptly evacuated and returned to Turkey.

The territories of Ardakhan, Kars and Batum will also be cleared without delay of Russian forces. . . .

ARTICLE 5. Russia will, without delay, proceed to demobilize her army, including those army units newly formed by her present government.

Moreover, Russia will either bring her warships into Russian ports and keep them there until general peace is concluded, or will disarm them at once. . . .

ARTICLE 6. Russia undertakes to conclude peace at once with the Ukrainian people's republic and to recognize the treaty of peace between the state and the powers of the Quadruple Alliance. The territory of the Ukraine must be, at once, cleared of Russian troops and the Russian Red Guard. Russia ceases all agitation or propaganda against the government or the public institutions of the Ukrainian people's republic.

Esthonia and Livonia must also be immediately cleared of Russian troops and the Russian Red Guard. . . .

Finland and the Aland Islands will also be, without delay, cleared of Russian troops and the Russian Red Guard and Finnish ports of the Russian fleet and of Russian naval forces. . . . Russia ceases all agitation or propaganda against the government or public institutions of Finland. . . .

ARTICLE 7. . . . the contracting parties bind themselves to respect the political and economic independence and the territorial inviolability of Persia and Afghanistan.

ARTICLE 8. The prisoners of war of both parties will be allowed to return home. . . .

ARTICLE 9. The contracting parties mutually renounce all indemnifications for their war expenses, that is, for government expenses for conducting the war, . . . including all requisitions made in the enemy's country.

ARTICLES 10-13. (These articles deal with technical matters.)

ARTICLE 14. The present peace treaty must be ratified. Exchange of ratification documents must take place in Berlin as soon as possible. The Russian Government binds itself to execute the exchange of ratification documents . . . in the course of two weeks. . . .

A SHORT BIBLIOGRAPHY

Carr, Edward Hallett, *The Bolshevik Revolution, 1917-1923* (New York, 1951-1953). 3 vols.
An extremely detailed and scholarly topical history of the revolution. The narrative history is completely omitted. One volume treats Communist theory and practice, the second, Soviet economics, and the third the international aspects.

Chamberlin, William Henry, *The Russian Revolution, 1917-1921* (New York, 1935). 2 vols.
The standard history of the revolution. Volume 2 covers the civil war period.

Chernov, Victor, *The Great Russian Revolution* (New Haven, 1936).
An account of the revolutionary events by a leading participant. Vivid and colorful, but seeks to justify the author's actions. Does not include the Bolshevik seizure of power.

Florinsky, M. T., *The Fall of the Russian Empire* (New Haven, 1931).
An excellent account of the collapse of the monarchy. Less effective in dealing with the Provisional Government.

Kerensky, Alexander, *The Catastrophe; Kerensky's Own Story of the Russian Revolution* (New York, London, 1927).
An interesting and revealing account seeking to justify the author's actions.

Reed, John, *Ten Days That Shook the World* (London, 1934; also American editions).
A vivid eye-witness account by an American radical present at the fall of the Provisional Government and the beginning of the Soviet regime.

Sukhanov, N. N., *The Russian Revolution, 1917; A Personal Record* (New York, 1955).
Another eye-witness account, by a radical socialist who was not radical enough to be a Bolshevik. Critical of both Right and Left.

Trotsky, Lev, *The History of the Russian Revolution* (New York, 1937). 3 vols. in 1.

A brilliant treatment of the revolution by the great Communist leader. Not especially tendentious, although sympathetic to the Soviets.

Warth, Robert D., *The Allies and the Russian Revolution* (Durham, N. C., 1954).

A sharply critical analysis of Allied policy and actions during the revolution. A scholarly treatment.

INDEX

VAN NOSTRAND ANVIL BOOKS already published